Terry Nation's
BLAKE'S 7

Acknowledgements

Thanks are due to a brave, select few who helped to make this book a reality. In no particular order, they are Clive Banks, for his diligent research on all matters studio and otherwise. Gary Russell, for advice in all matters pictorial, and for being a dedicated Servalan fan. Marcus Hearn, for advice in proving Blake's 7 was pukka after all, and Scott Gray and Gary Gillatt, for generally being Marvel bods.

My thanks also to Dave Sheppard, for his unending help and enthusiasm, Michael E. Briant, Anthony Brown, David Maloney, Anthony Clark, Caroline Batten, Alan Stevens, Kevin Davies, Gary Leigh and Shaun Sutton. And to Rod Green and Krystlyna Zukowska, for being there from the beginning.

From 'Luke Books': the incomparable Gary Shoefield, Sharon Shoefield and Luke Shoefield, Simon Carter and Paul Laurence.

Finally, to Richard Hollis, C. E. Banks, Andrew Skilleter and Jake Lingwood – the editor who survived it all – to Adrian Sington, Mr Waits, Kathy Dawn and her guitar, Rod Morgan and Bobbie, Margaret, Ali and the gang in 'C' Block. And not forgetting Mum, Nicola and Midge . . .

Terry Nation's BLAKE'S 7

Adrian Rigelsford

BOXTREE

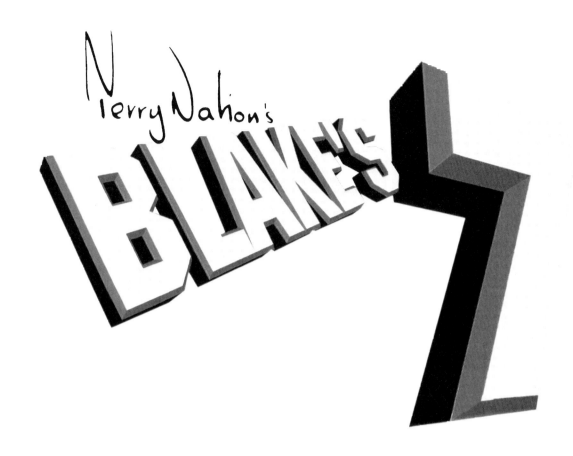

First published in the UK in 1995 by
Boxtree Ltd
Broadwall House
21 Broadwall
London SE1 9PL

1 2 3 4 5 6 7 8 9 10

Designed by PUSH, London
Printed and bound in the UK by Cambus Litho Ltd
Reprographics by Jade Reprographics Braintree, Essex

A CIP catalogue entry for this book is available from the
British Library

ISBN 0 7522 0891 8

Contents

Foreword by Terry Nation

Blake's Seven generates an enormous amount of print from both fans and professionals. I have read a good deal of this output, but this new manuscript is by far and away the most remarkable and brilliant piece of research I have ever seen; I am lost in admiration of the investigative skills of author Adrian Riglesford. His dogged determination shows through every section of the book. I had forgotten (or never knew) much of what the author has dug out of documents and the memories of the people who were part of turning 'B7' into a cult show. I might dispute certain nuances of some of those memories, particularly concerning character and artistic judgements. However my recall also may be flawed, coloured by self-ego and the classic insecurity that is part of the writers burden.

You will see that the logistics of preparing the first season became a nightmare. Nothing seemed to go as planned. The carefully worked out timetable became a house of cards that could tumble at any moment. Every foot of film and tape became vital. I've been asked why we never issued a reel of 'Bloopers', the out-takes of funny mistakes. The fact is that our 'Bloopers' were up there on the screen because re-takes were impossible.

Blake's Seven's first night was rapidly approaching and despite all, we were fairly confident that we had a good starting episode. (I have admitted since that if I had it to do over I would make a lot of changes). Our confidence was badly shaken when we took a look at a state of the art exhibition of special effects and model-making. The brilliant movie *Star Wars* appeared. I enjoyed and admired the film but came away from the screening green with envy. There was no way we could compete on the effect's level. It was clear that *Star Wars* had spent more on one short segment than the entire thirteen episode budget allowed 'B7'. I realized that we could not become a science fiction spectacular so we must aim at a different area. Our strengths had to come from our characters. They must be strong, must conflict, they must be ruthless, self-serving, ambitious and dangerous. I would write stories that were intriguing action adventures. All easier said than done, but that was the aim.

Meanwhile our penny-pinching FX tottered along. Space-craft jerked along hardly hidden wires. Going through a Black Hole meant a stage hand had to shake the scenery hard. When the *Liberator* crew had to land on an alien planet they seemed always to put down in a quarry near to the studios. These quarries must be the most over-used location in BBC history.

I cherish the legend about the 'B7' crew, transported down to the surface of a new planet. The director lined up his cameras and explained to the cast that they were being chased by some unseen merciless monsters. They were to run until they went out of sight around an angle in the cliff. The director called 'Action' and off they went, running like hell. As they reached the angle they came to an abrupt and bewildered halt as they collided with Dr Who and his companions coming from the other direction, pursued by the Daleks.

What follows is a book for the enthusiastic fan and the serious student of television. Enjoy it. I certainly did.

Terry Nation, Los Angeles.

Introduction

Blake's 7 was made at a time when television companies were not afraid to attempt science fiction. Nowadays, that genre has very much become a last resort, with crime thrillers and sitcoms leading the way, rather than anything set in outer space. Attitudes change though, and judging by the popularity of Star Trek – The Next Generation and The X Files, it seems that a new wave of fantasy series may well be on its way. But nothing surely will match Blake's 7 for its style and impact.

Today, some of the sets may look a bit unstable, and the costumes – with dated fashions patrolling across alien planets – well, perhaps a little outlandish, but the success the series experienced cannot be denied. This was not Star Trek, with the crew working as one. The passengers on the Liberator were frequently arguing and the threats they faced were far more tangible. Only occasionally did the series lapse into using monsters as such. The Federation, with its undeniable Nazi parallels, was an all too real, ever-present threat, and the heroes of the series were fallible.

These were not superhumans: they were just as susceptible to stun guns as anyone else, and were certainly shown to be mortal. Midway through the second series, Gan was crushed as a tunnel collapsed around him, and at the start of Season Four, Cally was killed in the blast of an explosion. They were portrayed as normal people, trying to overcome an enemy they could never beat, but one that they could certainly frustrate and annoy.

There is no analysis of the characters or their motivations in this book. Not everyone will share my opinion on those aspects. In any case, as the episodes are now available for purchase in video cassette form, it would be much better for the viewers to draw their own conclusions, and discover for themselves what made the crews of the Liberator and the Scorpio tick. Similarly, the special effects, costume designs, and so forth, are other vast areas to cover, and therefore, due to time and space, they also are not dealt with in this volume.

Rather this is an attempt to bring together the details of the actual physical task of making the show. We deal principally with when and where each episode was made, and the schedules that the production team faced in trying to get the finished programmes on television in time.

A basic guide to the making of Blake's 7, this book is intended primarily as a tribute to all those people, both in front of and behind the camera, who took Terry Nation's creation and turned it into the durable success that it undoubtedly became. Will it ever come back? That's not a question that can be answered within these pages, but just consider Star Trek. After the original series they said that it would never come back, and that if it did, it would fail. Look how many movies and spin-off series there have been to answer that point! So if the demand is there and the requests are loud enough, one day somebody somewhere might listen and turn once again to Blake's 7. At a time when such TV series as Maverick, Mission Impossible and The Prisoner are being revived for the big screen, who knows what could happen . . .

1 The Way Ahead

Towards the middle of the 1970s, as far as the BBC was concerned, when it came to writing science fiction Terry Nation could do no wrong. His formidable track record spoke for itself - the creation of the Daleks for *Doctor Who*, episodes of the acclaimed anthology series *Out of the Unknown*, a pilot episode for a series he planned called *The Incredible Robert Baldick*, and most recently of all, there was *Survivors*.

With Nation's ever-present concerns about the fate of mankind in the face of either atomic warfare or some environmental disaster, the Daleks were the mutated survivors of such a catastrophe. *Survivors* followed through the train of thought with a plot revolving around the consequences of a lethal virus that is accidentally released and wipes out 95 per cent of the human race as a result. That, though, was just the starting point.

The intention in *Survivors* was to show how the handful of humans left after the catastrophe formed into small communities, and had to start civilization again by quite literally going back to basics. Threats came, for example, from rogue groups trying to impose their own systems of martial law, and even from dogs - unfed and starving, former domesticated pets had now reverted to their pack instincts, roaming in groups and attacking any humans they came across.

Nation effectively created the series, and wrote most of the first thirteen episodes, with seven to his credit, while Jack Rodner and Clive Exton (writing as M. K. Jeeves, which is an ironic in-joke in a sense, as Exton would later go on to write the acclaimed *Jeeves & Wooster* series for Granada Television, starring Stephen Fry and Hugh Laurie) handled the remainder. The producer was Terence Dudley, fresh from completing *Doomwatch* in 1973.

Doomwatch, with its stories predicting environmental and scientific disasters that were all too plausible, had run for three seasons. Towards the end however, it lost the keen edge and shock values that had in part at least, led, in part at least, to its immense popularity with the viewers and its subsequent ratings success. To some extent this was due to the early departure of the series creators, Dr Kit Pedler and Gerry Davis - both veterans from the Patrick Troughton era of *Doctor Who* - as a result of creative differences with the production team. After they had gone, there was a noticeable change in the style and approach of the series. *Survivors* followed a similar course.

This series was commissioned in the first place to fill the gap left by *Doomwatch*. The BBC realized that there was a place in their viewing schedules for an 'adult' fantasy series that was more science fact than fiction, and Nation's concept met this need. The filming - which bravely moved from an initial phase of mixing studio recording work with location shooting to realizing all the material on video tape outdoors - took place throughout 1974 and into early 1975. The programme made its debut on 16 April 1975 and was an immediate success with

Blake's 7

critics and viewers alike. But while work was continuing on the final few episodes of the first season, Nation was already working on another idea for a new series, separate from *Survivors*.

By the time *Survivors* was commissioned for a second series, Nation was no longer directly involved in the writing of the episodes, and Dudley brought in many of his *Doomwatch* writers, such as Martin Worth, Roger Parkes and Don Shaw, to handle the new stories. By the time the third season was completed in 1977, it was stylistically quite different from its initial phase, and a proposed fourth season, which would have seen the English communities opening up communications via a ferry system with Holland and Amsterdam, was scrapped.

Once again there was a gap in the schedules for a fantasy series that would appeal to adult viewers, and without this time alienating younger viewers with strong themes and content, as had been the case with *Doomwatch* and *Survivors*. Fortunately, the ideal replacement was already waiting to be taken up, which Nation had been working on towards the end of his run on *Survivors*.

Earlier, during a meeting attended by various heads of the Drama Series department at the BBC, Nation had sold his idea for a series revolving around the exploits of '*The Dirty Dozen* in space'. The film in question that Nation referred to was made in 1967, and told of a group of soldiers, in prison for various crimes, who were given their freedom in order to make up a squad with a suicidal mission to attack a chateau held by the Nazis during the Second World War. It was a smash hit, and

Nation's idea of reworking the idea in an outer space setting won him a commission to write a pilot, followed by a contract to script all thirteen episodes of the proposed first season.

A producer adept at handling the technicalities of science fiction for television was now needed. The *Doctor Who* encampment was the obvious training ground for such a person and one of the more experienced directors from that particular programme would be ideal.

David Maloney had just finished work on the finale of *Doctor Who*'s fourteenth season, 'The Talons of Weng Chiang', the making of which had also been the subject of a Lively Arts documentary for BBC2 called 'Who's Doctor Who?'. During the past three seasons of the programme he had made four highly stylish and atmospheric stories, and as a result, was highly recommended in his field.

Maloney accepted the job on *Blake's 7*, and immediately asked the writer of *Talons* and the overall script editor of *Doctor Who*, Robert Holmes, to come and work for him in the same capacity on the new series. Holmes turned this offer down, as he was tired of being tied to a desk after three years spent on *Doctor Who* and wanted to return to freelance script writing on other programmes. He did, however, suggest Chris Boucher for the job.

Holmes had enjoyed working with Boucher on two stories he'd scripted for the fourteen season of *Doctor Who*, 'The Face of Evil' and 'The Robots of Death'. He had proved to be adept at handling different styles of science fiction, he was highly imaginative, and most importantly of all, he was very quick

Trevor Baxter as Professor Litefoot alongside Tom
Baker as the Doctor in 'The Talons of Weng Chiang',
the last *Doctor Who* story directed by David Maloney
before he moved on to produce Blake's 7.

when it came to rewrites. Maloney and Boucher met, and shortly afterwards, the writer was put under contract and started to work on the series. Holmes also promised to come and write for the series in the future if they wanted him to.

By the spring of 1977, Maloney was 'in office' and starting preproduction on a series that would have to be ready for broadcast by the new year. The task was a monumental one. Although there had been various science fiction series over the years - with *Doctor Who* being practically the grandfather of them all - *Blake's 7* would really stretch the resources of both the production team and the BBC. If it was going to succeed it would have to appeal to a mass audience, and not just to the minority who normally followed this type of series.

One of the first things that Maloney did, to help develop a uniform in-house style for the show, was to assemble a team of four directors who would handle all thirteen episodes. Rather than have a new director for each show, Maloney proposed a system whereby as each episode was finished, the director

working on that episode would immediately start work on another story. In the interim period while he had been editing and dubbing his first show, the other directors would be working along the same line and using the cast for location and studio work before they were needed again by the first director for his next story. To this end, Maloney called in former *Doctor Who* colleagues Michael E. Briant, Pennant Roberts and Douglas Camfield, while Vere Lorrimer came to the programme from elsewhere in the Drama Department.

With Boucher working on the scripts as they started to arrive in rapid succession, and the design department beginning to turn their sketches of the futuristic city and space ships for the first few stories into the props and scenery flats that would inhabit the studios of BBC TV Centre over the ensuing months, Maloney and his directors addressed what was perhaps the most important task of all - finding the six principal actors who would make up the human contingent of the '7'.

2 *Standard by Seven*

Gareth Thomas look distinctly un-Blake like in a restoration comedy during the early 1970s.

Opposite page: Gareth Thomas as Adam Brake in Children Of The Stones, the powerful children's fantasy series he completed prior to playing Blake.

By September 1977, the press carried the news that the BBC were about to start filming a new science fiction adventure series, and interest in the series began to build up rapidly before anything had even been committed to film, let alone rehearsed. A roll call was made of the actors who had been selected to play the leads, with Gareth Thomas confirmed as being signed up for the all-important pivotal role of Blake. The RADA-trained actor had won the role against competition from names such as Maurice Coulbourne, who would become a familiar face with the public in Philip Martin's seminal series, *Gangsters*, and in the early 1980s with *Howard's Way*, and Warren Clarke, whose background credits included playing one of the Droogs in Stanley Kubrick's infamous film adaption of Anthony Burgess's *A Clockwork Orange*.

Paul Darrow, who was also originally a contender for the part of Blake, won the part of Avon. With a career comprising theatre, television and radio work up until that point, Darrow was far from disappointed with this choice. Already it was clear from the content of the scripts for the first few episodes that the character of Avon had what could be described as a more 'enigmatic' quality than Blake, and would therefore be far more interesting to play.

Jenna, one of the two female leads in the series, went to Sally Knyvette, who had very little television work to her credit at that stage, and who was therefore delighted to win such a prime role in a potentially long-running series. The cast were being issued with contracts for enough episodes to fill two seasons, so there was some guarantee that at least two years' work would result from working on *Blake's 7* no matter what happened.

Michael Keating won the role of Vila, helped by a recommendation from Pennant Roberts, who had worked with him a few years earlier, casting him as Stephen Grigg in an episode of *Doomwatch* called 'Enquiry'. Also accustomed to working with Maloney in the past was David Jackson, who auditioned for and was given the part of Gan. Maloney recalls going to see Jackson in a play he was appearing in at the time, and seeing at the same time an actress in the cast called Jan Chappell. Although she had already auditioned unsuccessfully for the role of Jenna, Maloney was sufficiently impressed with her on this occasion to recall her and offer her the part of Cally.

Although Cally would not actually appear in the series until the fourth episode, Chappell was involved in the rehearsals and filming as soon as production on *Blake's 7* actually began in front of the cameras. Working with Briant, Roberts and Lorrimer, Maloney had structured a complex filming schedule for the first thirteen episodes which meant that filming, studio work and rehearsals for various episodes would all overlap.

Briant had been assigned the all-important first episode, 'The Way Back', which had undergone a title swap with the third episode 'Cygnus Alpha', on which Lorrimer handled the direction. Roberts had agreed to juggle the second and fourth episodes, 'Space Fall' and 'Time Squad', the latter featuring the debut of Cally.

As a result, Roberts was the first director to call the shots as the first few days of filming began for *Blake's 7* shooting location material for 'Time Squad' in Betchworth Quarry, before moving on to a vast, futuristic nuclear power station near Avon in Bristol. The series was at last underway, with just under four months to go before 'The Way Back' was

Sally Knyvette, Gareth Thomas and the security robot that was seen in several of the stories in the show's first year.

Michael Halsey as Varon and Pippa
Steel as Maja during studio rehearsals
for the first episode of *Blake's 7*-'The
Way Back'.

due to be screened. As soon as those sequences were
finished, Roberts had to backtrack and complete several big scenes for 'Space Fall' at the BBC's Ealing
film studio facility, where programmes were taken
for major special-effects sequences or action scenes
that could not be staged at TV Centre, needing, as
the BBC liked to call it, a 'controlled environment'
for recording.

Michael E. Briant then began shooting from the
first week of October over a seven-day period, as he
worked on the main exterior sequences for 'The Way
Back' - and immediately hit a problem thanks to a
lapse of memory. He recalls the fact that whilst he
was filming for a *Doctor Who* story called 'Revenge
of the Cybermen', he had taken a camera crew down
to the cave systems at Wookey Hole in the heart of
Somerset, and had made a mental note to return
there one day. The script for 'The Way Back' presented an ideal opportunity to do just that, but when he

took his production assistant there, they found the
caves were far smaller than he remembered, and he
had to shoot in the decidedly uncave-like tunnels of
a nearby MOD complex as an alternative.

As soon as Briant was finished, Lorrimer took
over the director's chair, and completed two days of
night filming in Rickmansworth Quarry for 'Cygnus
Apha'. From the following week, script read-
throughs and rehearsals for the studio material due
to be recorded at TV Centre began. Once again,
Roberts went first, and completed 'Space Fall' over
two days in studio at the beginning of November. Of
the 'Space Fall' cast apart from the regulars, Glyn
Owen and Norman Tipton were also held on contracts that secured their services until the end of the
month, as their characters carried over from 'Space
Fall' into the initial scenes of 'Cygnus Alpha'.

Although 'Space Fall' revolved around Blake's
first encounter with the ship that would feature

Robert James as Glynd during rehearsals for his appearance in 'The Way Back'.

Stephen Greif in 1978 when he was best known for his role as a South London gangster boss in the sitcom, Citizen Smith.

throughout the first three seasons of the series, the *Liberator*, none of the sequences involving the flight deck were recorded, as the complex set had not been completed in time. On 21 November, therefore, the first day of recording for 'Cygnus Alpha' there were two directors completing scenes from the studio control gallery with Lorrimer taking solo control for the following studio day to complete his episode. Briant had finished 'The Way Back' in between these two studio sessions, using a two-day recording period starting on 10 November, during which he staged the trial scenes where Blake was condemned and sent to the Cygnus Alpha penal colony.

Two months after he had actually begun shooting the story, Pennant Roberts now resumed work on 'Time Squad', with Jan Chappell, who had not been required for the intervening period, now returning full time with the cast. Unfortunately, the two days in studio did not go smoothly and a substantial amount of material remained unrecorded, so a remount would have to be staged at some point. By 2 December, when the second scheduled studio day allocated initially to 'Time Squad' was over, Briant and Lorrimer had both finished editing their

Brian Blessed as Vargas surrounded by
his followers in the derelict church-like
set of 'Cygnus Alpha'.

first episodes and were already working on the next episodes assigned to them.

For three days from 23 November onwards, Briant had worked with Darrow and Thomas from the principal cast in Black Park, in Buckinghamshire, famed as the site of so many climatic chases for the Hammer Horror films of the 1960s and early 1970s. 'The Web' marked the first time that anything which could technically be termed a 'monster' had been used in the series, featuring the Decimas, a race of genetically engineered drone creatures. There were quite a few robot guards, servants and computers seen through the course of the series, but comparatively few genuine 'creatures', and even then, they were nearly always humanoid in shape.

Lorrimer took the episode 'Seek-Locate-Destroy' for a couple of days' location work to the gas works in Fulham, on the outskirts of London, moving to Ealing for 'controlled' studio work for the following two days from 7 December. The character of Travis now made his debut, with Nation moulding his creation very much in the Sheriff of Nottingham mode.

Intended as the villainous opposition, Travis was quickly established as Blake's nemesis from the moment he made his debut. Stephen Greif, RADA trained like Thomas, was working on a BBC situation comedy, the fondly remembered *Citizen Smith*, when he heard that Maloney was having problems finding his 'Basil Rathbone' to match Thomas's 'Errol Flynn', and quickly put himself forward for consideration. After auditioning, Maloney asked him to join the regulars for a total of five appearances during the course of the rest of the season. The other character introduced in 'Seek-Locate-Destroy' was originally intended as a one-off appearance, but that idea was due to change rather quickly.

Servalan, as written by Nation, was initially intended as a male character, but 'he' somehow became 'she' during casting. Although Maloney recalls initially asking former Hammer Horror star Ingrid Pitt, of *Countess Dracula* and *The Vampire Lovers* fame, to join the cast for the few days she'd be required, the part was eventually awarded to another Hammer star, Jacqueline Pearce, who had played in *Plague of the Zombies* and *The Reptile*. She made such an impact with her performance that the possibility of bringing the character of Servalan back quickly became a certainty.

In a two-day recording session on 12-13 December, Briant completed all the scenes needed to finish 'The Web', before Thomas and Greif departed to start work on 'Duel' in the New Forest for four days from 14 December. This story marked the debut, and it would ultimately turn out, the solo appearance behind the cameras for the fourth director during Season One, Douglas Camfield. Camfield had a firmly established track record as an action director, his work on *The Professionals* and the hard-hitting *Target*, for example, winning great acclaim, so he was ideally suited for the episode in question, in which the main thrust of the story centred on Blake and Travis being forced into one-to-one combat. A point to note here is that although this was the seventh story recorded it was broadcast as the eighth in transmission order.

Before a brief break for Christmas, Roberts finished off 'Seek-Locate-Destroy' from 22 to 23 December. A brief period of studio time was also taken up with the scenes that remained uncompleted from 'Time Squad', allowing him to finish the editing of that episode with very little time to spare

before it was actually broadcast.

The new year started with 'The Way Back' being screened on 2 January on BBC1, 'Duel' rehearsing for the complex studio work it required, and filming at Ealing starting on the 3 January for a three-day session on the next tale, 'Mission to Destiny', with Roberts again directing. 'Duel' went before the studio cameras for two days on 9 January, but Camfield fell into the same trap as Roberts and was unable to complete the scenes he needed in the allocated time. Michael E. Briant stepped forward and offered him some time in his next studio block, during 'Project Avalon', which he had already started filming as Camfield finished at TV Centre.

It's quite ironic that Briant once again had to find a cave system to film the scenes for his third episode of the season. This time, however, Wookey Hole was ideal, and from 10 January he based the four days of shooting he had to complete around that area of Somerset. Thomas only arrived on the second day of shooting along with Greif, as they had

The *Liberator's* crew wore special suits such as the one worn here by Paul Darrow as Avon, in order to survive on planets with a sub-zero surface temperature.

Sally Knyvette as Jenna seated at
one of the controls of the *Liberator*
flight deck.

both been held up in an overlap of the studio sessions for 'Duel'. With Servalan now established as the villainess, Jacqueline Pearce was also required over these dates. Maloney was happy to run her appearances alongside Greif's, for the two characters made ideal venomous sparring partners.

On returning to London, the principal cast assembled to finish 'Mission to Destiny', with the studio sequences completed under Roberts' direction. A couple of days later, Vere Lorrimer began three days of shooting at Ealing for 'Breakdown', an episode that for once revolved around Gan, a character David Jackson felt had been woefully underused up until that point. It is evident, however, that 'Breakdown' was one of the scripts from the latter stages of Season One to suffer from the fact that time was quite literally running out.

Any writer would surely flinch at the thought of having to complete thirteen packed episodes of television drama on their own, but Nation had not shied away from this considerable challenge and had tackled the job head on. Nevertheless, in consequence, with the end of the series now in sight, it would be fair to say that the three or four scripts immediately prior to the interlinked final two episodes suffered as a result of the concentrated schedule.

All the story threads that had been presented for the first eleven episodes had to be tied up to the satisfaction not only of the BBC, but also of the viewers. Thus with 'Breakdown', for example, the scripts were underrunning in length due to the fact that Nation was hard at work completing 'Deliverence' and 'Orac' to round the season off. Chris Boucher was now regularly working with the directors to expand and add to the scripts in order to bring them up to time, with ideas being welcomed from the actors as well during the rehearsals to help with the situation.

By 30 January, the two-day studio session that Briant needed to complete 'Project Avalon' had begun, and Camfield returned to use the time he had been allocated across these dates to finish 'Duel', just under three weeks from broadcast. The script problem arose again on 'Bounty' for Pennant Roberts, which had to have a lot of additional work carried out on scenes and dialogue by both the director and Boucher before the principals arrived for the story's main location work, which covered

Paul Darrow and Paul Keating get used to the *Liberator's* teleport control console.

The *Liberator* crew explore the soon-to-be re-activated launch pad control room in 'Deliverance'.

three days' filming in Quex Park in Kent, from 1 February onwards. A small amount of material remained outstanding, and Roberts finished this back at Black Park in Buckinghamshire on 7 February.

Studio work on 'Breakdown' was finished by Lorrimer following two days of work on 11-12 February. The broadcast dates were now getting closer and closer. The last thing that Maloney needed was to lose one of his scheduled directors, but this is exactly what happened.

Nation had now finished 'Deliverence', and Douglas Camfield was committed to the project as the episode's director, but a conflict of schedules with his next series at the BBC meant he was unavailable for the dates in question. Roberts was still heavily occupied in editing and dubbing 'Bounty', and Lorrimer was at work on extensive pre-production work that had to be carried out on the season's finale 'Orac', so the most obvious move was to ask Michael E. Briant to come back. Maloney now hit another problem, however, as Briant was finishing off work on another series and could not meet the filming dates for the location work, but was happy to handle the two-day studio block. Maloney therefore had no alternative but to step behind the camera himself.

His brief return to directing was not a pleasur-

able experience though, as both cast and crew alike recall that the three days spent in Betchworth Quarry from 13 February onwards were some of the coldest that year. And with many of the extras wearing nothing but animal skins to protect them against the freezing weather, everyone was very glad indeed to get back inside the warm studios at TV Centre.

Roberts moved into the studio five days later for the remainder of 'Bounty', with the time between location filming and the two-day session from 20 February having allowed more work to be done on expanding the script with Boucher. Exterior filming and studio recording once again overlapped. Lorrimer started shooting 'Orac' around the Springwell Lock Quarry for five days from 20 February, with both Pearce and Greif, returning for the final two episodes, working on their material for the first day before Thomas and the rest of the principals arrived on the second.

Michael E. Briant returned to plan out the studio work needed for 'Deliverance' at this point, and that started as the cast returned, with the penultimate two-day session for the season running across 2-3 March. The end was now in sight as Lorrimer began rehearsals for the scenes that had to be finished, not only 'Orac', but for the Season as a whole, but once again, things did not run as smoothly as they'd been planned.

In the gap between finishing the location work and starting on the studio sequences, Stephen Greif had a bad accident playing squash, snapping his Achilles tendon. The injury was such that there was no possibility that he would be able to finish the scenes for 'Orac', so with no time to reshoot and recasting being a total impossibility, Lorrimer had to revert to clever camera angles in order to hide the fact that the Travis scene in the studio was not Greif but an extra doubling for him. By fast-cutting the sequences, so that the audience would have no time to guess the difference, and getting Greif to dub dialogue in postproduction, the illusion was complete, and only those who worked on the episode and knew the situation would have noticed.

'Orac' was finished on 15 March after two days in studio, and the episode went out on BBC1 on 27 March, a mere twelve days later! Whatever the circumstances, the series had proved to be a resounding success. Even though 'The Way Back' debut had a disappointing 7.4 million viewers, and 'Space Fall' had logged an even lower audience than that, by the time 'Cygnus Alpha' was screened, the reputation of the series was beginning to spread. The figures quickly began to reach the 9 million mark and head towards the all-important 10 million figure. 'Seek-Locate-Destroy' actually hit an all-time high for the series as a whole, with 10.9 million viewers, while 'Orac' came a close second as the season's finale, with 10.6 million. Nation, Maloney and Boucher had a sizeable hit on their hands.

Although broadcasting had finished, work was already underway for the payoff sequel to the cliffhanger that had been set up by Nation with 'Orac'. He had actually started work on drafting the ideas for the first story of Season Two midway through production on the early episodes of Season One towards the end of 1977. The BBC were that confident that they would have a hit on their hands, and they were right. Merchandise started to appear quite quickly, and there was a demand for the record release of Dudley Simpson's rousing theme tune.

Simpson had working on practically all the incidental music for the series so far - the sole exception to date being Douglas Camfield's 'Duel' - and would go on to score the soundtracks for all of the ensuing episodes except 'Gambit' towards the end of Season Two, which Elizabeth Parker would oversee.

That was not the only change to take place during the second year of the series. It had become clear that the pressure on Nation during the course of the first year, in which he had had to write every story,

Carinthia West as Tyce and T.P. McKenna as Sarkoff in a break during the shooting of 'Bounty'.

Thomas and Chappell on the set of Sarkoff's palatial retreat in 'Bounty'. The set was full of 'antiques' from the 20th Century.

The set of the *Liberator* was a popular place for the cast to relax in between shots.

had been intense, and moves were made to bring in some other writers to share the burden for the next batch of thirteen episodes. One of the first approached involved the writer in question keeping a promise he had made to Nation, and that was Robert Holmes.

Like the cast, Maloney and Boucher were under contract for twenty-six episodes, so they would definitely be staying with the show, but out of the four directors involved with Season One, only Vere Lorrimer stayed. Briant and Roberts moved elsewhere in the drama department, whilst Camfield began to steer clear of science fiction altogether. Having worked on dozens of episodes of *Doctor Who* since the series had begun, he freely admitted that he did not want to become tied down to another long-running science fiction series, and he too moved on. So Maloney would have to find a new team of directors to work with. However, while there were a number of new faces behind the scenes, those on screen would remain the same - but not for long . . .

3 *Blake's 7*
Episode Guide

Introduction

With four seasons, fifty-two episodes and close to forty-five hours of screen time to its credit, *Blake's 7* certainly has a considerable number of plotlines to its name. This chapter is a basic material guide to Season One, and there are also one of two general points to note for the uninitiated.

The writer, director and basic cast and production credits are noted with each episode. Broadcast dates and the general time slots that the series was screened in are also stated.

Each tale had its own production code number, and that system ran as follows. Each season was denoted by a letter of the alphabet, with each story given a number for its position in the broadcast order of the stories. 'Cygnus Alpha', for example, was the third story of Season One, and therefore has the code of 'A3', whereas 'Blake', the final episode of Series Four and the finale for the series as a whole, has the code of 'D13'.

Any additional data, such as uncredited work by directors or writers, is also detailed. Stories that acted as part of any of the *Blake's 7* fiction that has been published have that information noted at the end of their synopsis.

Season One

Regular Cast Members
Blake – Gareth Thomas
Jenna – Sally Knyvette
Vila – Michael Keating
Avon (Stories A2-A13) – Paul Darrow
Gan (Stories A2-A13) – David Jackson
Cally (Stories A4-A13) – Jan Chappell
Voice of Zen (Stories A3-A13) – Peter Tuddenham
Servalan (A6, A9, A12-A13) – Jacqueline Pearce
Travis (Stories A6, A8, A9, A12-A13) – Stephen Grief

Regular Production Team
Producer – David Maloney
Script Editor – Chris Boucher

Pippa Steel starred as Maja in
'The Way Back'.

A1. The Way Back
Written by Terry Nation.

On the Earth of the distant future, Roj Blake begins to find his 'reprogramming' is failing. The former resistance leader was caught, brainwashed and given a new identity by the ruling dictatorship, the Federation, only now his memory is returning. Put on trial, and framed for gross molestation charges, he is sentenced to spend the rest of his life on the penal colony of Cygnus Alpha.

Bran Foster – Robert Beatty
Glynd – Robert James
Varon – Michael Halsey
Maja – Pippa Steel
Richie – Alan Butler
Tarrant – Jeremy Wilkin
Ravella – Gillian Bailey
Arbiter – Margaret John
Doctor Havant – Peter Williams
Alta Morag – Susan Field
Director – Michael E. Briant
Designer – Martin Collins
Broadcast: 2 January 1978 1800 – 1850hrs
Novelized by Trevor Hoyle in *Blake's 7*.

A2: Space Fall
Written by Terry Nation.

On board a prison ship bound for Cygnus Alpha, Blake's attempted mutiny is vanquished, but the arrival of a mysterious, gigantic vessel provides a use for the mutineers. Blake, along with fellow convicts Avon and Jenna, are sent on board, but the ship does not prove to be that easy to board . . .

Commander Leylan – Glyn Owen
Sub-Commander Raiker – Leslie Schofield
Artix – Norman Tipton
Teague – David Hayward
Nova – Tom Kelly
Dainer – Michael Mackenzie
Krell – Brett Forrest
Garton – Bill Weston
Wallace – Clinton Morris
Director – Pennant Roberts
Designer – Roger Murray-Leach
Broadcast: 9 January 1978 1915-2010hrs
Novelized by Trevor Hoyle in *Blake's 7*.

A3: Cygnus Alpha
Written by Terry Nation.

Blake, Avon and Jenna are heading towards Cygnus Alpha in the spaceship, which projects its name, the *Liberator*, into Jenna's mind, to try and rescue the convicts from the prison ship. They find the *Liberator* is equipped with weapons, a teleport system and an onboard computer called Zen. When Blake beams down to the planet, he's captured and taken to Vargas, who rules Cygnus Alpha like a religious cult, and demands that he hands over the *Liberator*.

Vargas – Brian Blessed
Kara – Pamela Salem
Commander Leylan – Glyn Owen
Artix – Norman Tipton
Arco – Peter Childs
Laran – Robert Russell
Selman – David Ryall
Director – Vere Lorrimer
Designer – Robert Berk
Broadcast: 16 January 1978 1915-2010hrs
Novelized by Trevor Hoyle in *Blake's 7*.

A4: Time Squad
Written by Terry Nation.

The *Liberator* heads for Saurian Major, one of the Federation's communications bases, which Blake intends to destroy. A distress signal is detected, and the ship takes on board a mysterious capsule, containing cryogenic pods. On the planet's surface, Blake's initial confrontation with Cally, an Auron with telepathic powers, becomes an alliance as they join forces to stage his attack. Meanwhile, on the *Liberator*, the inhabitants of the cryogenic pods start to come to life, seemingly intent on killing all of the crew.

Alien – Tony Smart
Alien – Mark McBride
Alien – Frank Henson
Director – Pennant Roberts
Designer – Roger Murray-Leach
Broadcast: 23 January 1978 1915-2010hrs
Novelized by Trevor Hoyle in *Blake's 7*.

The *Liberator* flight deck set took up so much studio space that it could not be erected for every studio session. Sequences were often filmed for several episodes on the same day.

A5: The Web
Written by Terry Nation.

Cally has now joined the crew of the *Liberator*, and immediately starts to try and sabotage the ship, which becomes trapped in a mysterious weblike net drifting around the orbit of a planet. It becomes clear that some form of psychic attack has brought them there, and Blake teleports to the surface to investigate. Blake finds the last survivors of an experimental project set up on the planet to develop and experiment with genetic engineering. They are one of two species present, the others are the Decimas, dronelike creatures who are running out of control. The scientists are outlawed members of Cally's race, hence their ability to manipulate Cally telepathically to send the ship off course to their world, and refuse to free the *Liberator* from the web until Blake hands over power cells that will enable them to destroy the Decimas.

Novara – Miles Fothergill
Geela – Ania Marson
Saymon – Richard Beale
Decimas – Deep Roy
Willie Sheara, Gilda Cohen, Ismet Hassm
Marcus Powell, Molly Tweedley
Director – Michael E. Briant
Designer – Martin Collins

Broadcast: 30 January 1978 1915-2010hrs

A6: Seek-Locate-Destroy
Written by Terry Nation.

Blake stages a sabotage attack on the planet Centero's Federation communications base, but it goes wrong and Cally is trapped on the debris and left behind as the bombs the *Liberator* crew set up detonate. In the Federation's space headquarters, Supreme Commander Servalan gives Space Commander Travis, who Blake thought he had killed years ago, a mission to seek, locate and destroy Blake. Travis arrives on Centero and sets an elaborate trap, with Cally as bait.

Rontane – Peter Miles
Prell – Peter Craze
Escon – Ian Cullen
Bercol – John Bryans
Rai – Ian Oliver
Eldon – Astley Jones
Director – Vere Lorrimer
Designer – Robert Berk
Broadcast: 6 February 1978 1915-2010hrs
Novelized by Trevor Hoyle in *Blake's 7 - Project Avalon.*

A group shot of the Decimas, the creatures who were to storm the laboratory in 'The Web'.

Blake confronts the mutated form of
Sayman in the research centre run by
outlawed members of Cally's race in 'The
Web'.

A7: Mission to Destiny
Written by Terry Nation.

The *Liberator* encounters a cruiser called the *Ortega*, and Blake, Avon and Cally find the crew have been knocked out with a gas on board. One of their number, Dortmunn, is missing, as is one of the ship's escape pods, so it's assumed he was responsible. The ship is carrying a neurotrope energy refractor, vital to save the planet Destiny from a deadly fungus. In an attempt to help, Blake sets off to take the device there on the *Liberator*, while Avon and Cally stay on the *Ortega* to repair Dortmunn's sabotage, but when they find his murdered body, they realize that not everything is as it appears.

Kendall – Barry Jackson
Sara – Beth Morris
Mandrian – Stephen Tate
Sonheim – Nigel Humphreys
Grovane – Carl Forgione
Levett – Kate Coleridge
Pasco – John Leeson
Rafford – Brian Capron
Dortmunn – Stuart Fell
Director – Pennant Roberts
Designer – Martin Collins
Broadcast: 13 February 1978 1915-2010hrs

A7: Duel
Written by Terry Nation.

The powerful survivors of a race devastated by centuries of war stop the *Liberator* as it is about to ram Travis's ship, and Blake and Travis are brought down to the planet, where the young woman Sinofar, and the old hag Giroc, force them to engage in combat to the death, so that they may learn about the human race. Blake, accompanied by Jenna, and Travis, with a sole Mutoid, a genetically altered human who thrives on blood serum, find themselves in a forest wilderness, where it is genuinely a case of survival of the fittest.

Sinofar – Isla Blair
Giroc – Patsy Smart
Mutoid – Carol Royle
Director – Douglas Camfield
Designer – Roger Murray-Leach
Broadcast: 20 February 1978 1915-2010hrs
Novelized by Trevor Hoyle in *Blake's 7 - Project Avalon*.

President Sarkoff of the planet Lindor was targetted by Blake as a candidate for preventing the spread of the Federation.

A9: Project Avalon
Written by Terry Nation.

On an ice planet, Travis massacres a group of rebels and captures their leader, Avalon. Blake, due to meet with the group, meets the lone survivor, Chevner, who explains what happened. Knowing full well that Blake will attempt to rescue Avalon, Travis shows Servalan his plague-carrying android replica of her, which he plans to use to wipe out the crew of the *Liberator* and take over the ship.

Avalon – Julia Vidler
Chevner – David Bailie
Terloc – John Rolfe
Mutoid – Glynis Barber
Scientist – John Baker
Guard – David Sterne
Guard – Mark Holmes
Director – Michael E. Briant
Designer – Chris Pemsel
Broadcast: 27 February 1978 1915-2010hrs
Novelized by Trevor Hoyle in *Blake's 7 - Project Avalon*.

A10: Breakdown
Written by Terry Nation.

The *Liberator* enters a meteorite storm, which causes a malfunction with the limiter implant in Gan's skull, sending him on a rampage which Blake and the others are barely able to stop. At the Space Laboratory XK.72, Professor Kayn realizes that something is wrong as such devices are only implanted in the minds of dangerous criminals, and alerts the Federation to the presence of Blake's ship.

Professor Kayn – Julian Glover
Farren – Ian Thompson
Renor – Christian Roberts
Director – Vere Lorrimer
Designer – Peter Brachacki
Broadcast: 6 March 1978 1915-2010hrs

A11: Bounty
Written by Terry Nation.

Blake and Cally infiltrate Federation security to reach the retreat of President Sarkoff, the exiled leader of the planet Lindor, who Blake tries to talk into returning to that planet to rally his race, and stop the inevitable civil war that would leave the way open for the Federation to take over his world. The *Liberator* picks up a distress signal from what appears to be an abandoned craft, and Gan is tricked into beaming on board a team of bounty hunters. When Blake, Cally, Sarkoff and his assistant teleport on board, they find that Avon and the rest of the crew are gone.

Sarkoff – T. P. McKenna
Tyce – Carinthia West

Knyvette and Darrow share a joke between takes during a recording session

Tarvin – Marc Zuber
Cheney – Mark York
Amagon Guard – Branche
Director – Pennant Roberts
Designer – Roger Murray-Leach
Broadcast: 13 March 1978 1915-2010hrs

A12: Deliverance
Written by Terry Nation.

Servalan monitors a small craft at Space Command, which the *Liberator* sees catch fire and sends a search party to find the survivors who ejected in escape pods. They find Ensor, a badly injured man who is trying to transport micropower cells to his Father, which are vital for his survival. He speaks of his Father's incredible invention, Orac, and the power that it could bring to anyone who possesses it.

Ensor – Tony Caunter
Meegat – Susan Farmer
Maryatt – James Lister
Directors – (Studio material) Michael E. Briant
(Uncredited location work) David Maloney
Designer – Robert Berk
Broadcast: 20 March 1978 1915-2010hrs
Novelized by Trevor Hoyle in *Blake's 7 - Project Avalon.*

A13: Orac
Written by Terry Nation.

With Ensor dead, the *Liberator* heads for his Father's home on Aristo, in the desperate hope that there will be medical supplies there, as Gan, Jenna, Avon and Vila have all contracted radiation sickness. Travis and Servalan have reached the planet already, in their quest for Orac, but fail to gain access as easily to Ensor senior's base as Blake and Cally do. Ensor is a computer genius, and the fruition of his lifetime's work is Orac, a compact computer, imbued with incredible abilities and Ensor's cantankerous personality, but the scientist's mechanical heart is failing. Blake and Cally have to get him to the *Liberator* to perform the surgery needed to replace the failing micropower cells, but it's then that Travis and Servalan arrive.

Season Cliffhanger
Orac projects a future prediction on Zen's screen, showing the *Liberator* exploding as it's destroyed.

Ensor – Derek Farr
Phibians – Paul Kidd, James Muir
Voice of Orac – Derek Farr
Director – Vere Lorrimer
Designer – Martin Collins
Broadcast: 27 March 1978 1905-2000hrs
Novelized by Trevor Hoyle in *Blake's 7 - Project Avalon.*

Brian Croucher was to replace Stephen Greif as Travis, who was unable to return for the second season of *Blake's 7*.

4 The Search for a Star...

It was only a matter of four months or so before the principal cast of *Blake's 7* found themselves back at the Acton Rehearsal Rooms - affectionately known as the 'Acton Hilton' due to the fact that the front of the building looks as if it was designed as a hotel - blocking out the scripts for the initial episodes that would make up the second season of the programme. There were, however, one or two changes, both in front of and behind the camera.

One decision that had been made principally as soon as Chris Boucher started commissioning the new stories was to keep Servalan and Travis as the main opposition to the crew of the *Liberator*. Jacqueline Pearce had agreed to reprise the role indefinitely, but Stephen Greif declined. Since that time Greif has stated that he had by then grown tired of the role, and felt that it was not achieving the full potential of the Travis character. Whatever the reason, he left the programme and David Maloney had to recast the part. Brian Croucher was signed up, and would appear in eight episodes during the course of Season Two, alongside Pearce.

Behind the scenes, Maloney had drawn up plans for a different recording system to that employed for the first year's stories. The new season would effectively be divided into two halves, of six and seven episodes respectively. For the first block of six adventures, three directors would be given two stories each. All the material that needed location work would be shot before any studio work had begun. After that, the directors would take turns to move into TV Centre and complete the interior scenes for each instalment.

As soon as production of the first half was completed, the second batch of episodes would be recorded using the same set-up, again with three directors taking two stories each. As it turned out, Maloney himself would end up directing the seventh and final episode for the year. Because he knew the programme well, Vere Lorrimer was given the first two episodes to get things started. Two directors who were new to the programme - Jonathan Wright-Miller and George Spenton-Foster - would then take on two scripts each.

The scripts for Lorrimer were by Terry Nation and Robert Holmes, with Nation's 'Redemption' taking up the story from the cliffhanger at the end of Season One, while Holmes' story, 'Killer', was a more

general adventure for the season. Both needed extensive location shooting, and following a brief rehearsal period, the cast and crew moved down to a nuclear power station at Oldbury near Avon, which, apart from having featured in Pennant Roberts' 'Time Squad' during the previous year, had also been used by the *Doctor Who* production team on a story called 'The Hand of Fear'. Lorrimer had four days there in total, and logically opted to spend two days on 'Redemption', from 31 July, and then started work on 'Killer' from 2 August. A few days later, the cast joined Jonathan Wright-Miller as he began shooting exterior material for the first of his episodes, 'Shadow', which was the first story to be broadcast under Chris Boucher's name. Miller spent three days from 7 August onwards, in and around some sandpits in Dorset completing material, before moving to Gloucestershire on 10 August for another three days work around Clearwell Scowles - with its lush vegetation a stark contrast to the gravel of Dorset - shooting the sequences needed for 'Horizon', a script that had been completed by Allan Prior, a veteran of many crime series such as *Z-Cars* and *Softly, Softly.*

George Spenton-Foster had selected a vast laboratory complex in Oxford, and, working with his production assistant, scouted the area for other suitable locations so that his work could be centred around the same area for the six days of filming he began as soon as Miller had finished with the cast on his shows. Foster's scripts were 'Weapon', another script by Boucher, and 'Pressure Point', the second story to be completed by Nation that year.

The complex Foster used on 14-16 August was the Rutherford Laboratories. While locations were finalized for the next few days for 'Pressure Point', the cast returned to London and completed material that had to be staged at the BBC studio facilities in Ealing, with Vere Lorrimer behind the cameras working on 'Redemption' from 17 to 18 August. They then returned to Oxford and began three days of filming from 21 August in and around Abingdon.

Foster's two stories were actually the first episodes of the season to feature Travis and Servalan, with Brian Croucher making his debut.

Gareth Thomas with Souad Faress as Selma and Darien Angadi as Ro, rehearsing on one of the sets built for 'Horizon'.

The Travis costume had been modified and redesigned between seasons. Previously Greif had made clear his discomfort at wearing the original heavy leather suit under the intense heat of the studio lighting, so Croucher's new outfit was made of a much lighter material, although it was still quite cumbersome to move around in.

By 23 August, all the location material that had been planned for the first six stories was effectively 'in the can'. Back in London, studio rehearsals began. Foster had to backtrack slightly and move into the studios first to work on 'Weapon' between 28 and 29 August, completing all except the scenes on the bridge of the *Liberator*. The set was still proving to be a problem, as it required a vast amount of studio space and it was not logistically sound to use it for every recording session. As with Season One, scenes from several episodes were recorded on the set over one day to save on time and money. Those for both 'Weapon' and 'Pressure Point' were done on 30 September.

Lorrimer was now waiting to use the cast to finish 'Redemption', which took two days to complete from 8 September. He immediately started rehearsals after that point on the studio material for 'Killer', which moved into TV Centre ten days later, spending two days there from 19 to 20 September. Once again, the *Liberator* scenes remained unrecorded, and these would have to wait for some two months before they were actually recorded.

Foster was now back, and had started planning out the remaining scenes for 'Pressure Point', which followed on from the work he had done at the end of September. This work was recorded at TV Centre over 10-11 October. With Lorrimer and Foster now editing and dubbing their episodes, it remained for Miller to move in and complete the first cycle of six stories.

'Horizon' was finished between 20 and 21 October, with only the *Liberator* sequences unrecorded, and they were finished in the first week of November, as the last scenes of 'Shadow' were also completed. This point also marked the final appearance in the series for David Jackson's character of Gan, for the actor had become unhappy with the restrictions placed on the development of his

David Jackson stands alone on the deck of the *Liberator* during one of his last studio sessions as Gan, who was to be killed off at the climax of 'Pressure Point'.

A full view of the *Liberator* set, with the flight control seats for the crew and the corridor to the right leading to their quarters.

Opposite page: The incomparable Jacqueline Pearce as Servalan in the costume she wore during 'The Harvest Of Kairos'.

role, which had not turned out as he had hoped initially. It is a very rare move for one of the characters in a long-running series such as *Blake's 7* to be killed off as Gan was, with the corridor collapsing around him in 'Pressure Point's climactic scenes, but he was given a heroic end, and structurally it gave Boucher an ideal opportunity to incorporate tension amongst the remaining characters as they tried to blame his death on each other.

The final scenes for the first six episodes involved *Liberator* material for 'Killer', which Lorrimer staged from 8 to 9 December, and with Jackson absent from all recording sessions for that particular episode. In order, the sequence of the stories for the first half of Season Two now ran as 'Redemption' first, followed by 'Shadow', 'Weapon', 'Horizon' and 'Pressure Point' in that order. 'Killer' was moved to the seventh episode in the season, with 'Trial' yet to be recorded, slotting in at number six.

Another minor change in the cast occurred with the computer, Orac, which was proving to be an ideal verbal sparring partner for Darrow and Keating in the scripts. Derek Farr had made it clear that he did not want to return as a mere 'voice artiste' for the

duration of Season Two, so Maloney gave the job of vocalizing the irritable computer to Peter Tuddenham, who had remained as Zen's voice all along.

With Season Two's start date for broadcast now confirmed as being in the first week of January, work began on the second batch, this time of seven episodes, to complete the run of thirteen stories, again using the new work system that Maloney had implemented.

Work had actually already begun by the time Lorrimer was finishing 'Killer', with director Derek Martinus starting location work just over a week after 'Shadow' had been completed. The three directors now sharing this batch of seven episodes were again Lorrimer and Foster, with Martinus now joining the team when Miller moved on to other projects. It is worth noting that Lorrimer had agreed to direct three episodes out of the seven, including the season's finale, but this was not to be.

Like Maloney, Martinus had extensive experience with science fiction from working on *Doctor Who*, and actually used a location for 'Trial', with the script yet again by Chris Boucher, that Maloney had

used a couple of years before. This site was the Royal Alexander and Albert School in Surrey, which had been one of the key locations for Maloney's 'The Deadly Assassin' on *Doctor Who*, and Martinus shot there for two days on 13 and 14 November, with only Gareth Thomas needed out of the main cast for these sequences.

As soon as this was finished, the cast were once again assembled in Betchworth Quarry, with Vere Lorrimer staging scenes from Allan Prior's script, 'Hostage'. One of the guest cast in this episode was to be the veteran character actor Duncan Lamont, but tragically he died shortly after this location work was completed. There was no way the production team could work his completed scenes into the plot without the studio material his character was required for, so Lorrimer had no choice other than to stage a remount of the key location scenes that had involved Lamont just prior to carrying out the main studio work for this episode, using a different actor in the part.

Lorrimer was effectively making 'Hostage' and 'Countdown' - the third and final script for the season, written by Terry Nation - back to back as far as the location material was concerned. Therefore work began on the second of those stories for three days from 27 to 29 November at the Ealing Studios. In between though, several scenes for 'Voice from the Past', with Foster working on a script by Roger Parkes, had been mounted at the Wembley Conference Centre on 23-24 November.

Remembering the area from their work on 'Horizon', the crew returned to Gloucestershire for three days for 'The Keeper'. This penultimate story for Season Two was directed by Martinus at Bream Scowles from Allan Prior's script between 4 and 6 December. It was immediately after this that the cast returned to London to finish 'Killer'.

'The Keeper' was written very quickly as a replacement for the proposed two-part story that Terry Nation was due to write for the season's finale. Other commitments eventually prevented Nation from fulfilling this task, so Prior was given the job. This story involved bringing to a climax the *Liberator's* search for clues to the location of the Achilles heel of the Federation, Star One, the automatic computer control centre behind all that organization's operations. This would allow Boucher to actually take the *Liberator's* crew to Star One in the final story of the season.

Bruce Purchase as Gloa with the trapped Sally Knyvette as Jenna in 'The Keeper'.

As with *Doctor Who* - or indeed any series - there were a number of casualties between script and screen, with one such victim being the story, 'Death Squad' by Pip and Jane Baker. This story actually got as far as being scheduled for filming, but the costs involved proved to be prohibitive, and the script was abandoned at the last minute. A planned script for Season Three by Robert Holmes met the same fate, as did one for Season Four by Graham Williams, with even Paul Darrow himself getting as far as completing a script, titled 'Man of Iron', before that was finally shelved. Since they were never made into episodes, the quality of these discarded scripts cannot be judged, but certainly Boucher would never have commissioned them in the first place if he did not think the story would work. As it is, problems of money and time were invariably the real reasons behind the decision to drop these scripts.

One of the last sections of filming to be carried out before studio recording began was for Robert Holmes's second script that year, 'Gambit', with Foster again directing. Two days, 21 and 22 December, were spent working around the lower depths of the Royal Festival Hall's labyrinth of concrete tunnels.

Immediately after Christmas, on 28-29 December, Martinus started work on the studio material for 'Trial', with the *Liberator* scenes again being left until a later date. These missing scenes would be staged on 10 January, with Lorrimer then taking over on 11 January and starting the scenes for 'Hostage' and 'Countdown' that involved the *Liberator* bridge. The two days following that were concentrated on the remainder of the script that had not been completed for 'Hostage'.

On 9 January, following on from a repeat of 'Orac' the week before, 'Redemption' started off Season Two on screen on BBC1, with a respectable 'opening night' viewing figure of just under 8 million viewers. With broadcasting now underway, time was beginning to catch up with the production team.

By this time 'Countdown' was in rehearsal, and moved to TV Centre for two consecutive days of studio recording from 23 to 24 January. Lorrimer now started editing his two episodes, while Foster also moved in to complete his. 'Voice from the Past' had a longer period in studio than normal, with a three-day taping session lasting from 1 to 3 February. Ten days later, Foster moved the cast in for 'Gambit', with the *Liberator* sequences required for that story on the flight deck already completed during the studio time in the previous recording block. The elaborate casino footage and all other material set around Freedom City was completed during 13-14 February.

The first eleven episodes were now either complete or nearing completion. Martinus returned to shoot the interior scenes for 'The Keeper' at the end of the month, again using a three-day studio session between 22 and 24 February. While he was editing, Lorrimer was meant to start work on the final script's preproduction. But as with 'Deliverance' the season before, Maloney suddenly found himself without a director when Lorrimer proved to be unavailable for the dates he was required. As a result, Maloney once again stepped in and directed, as he had done the previous year, without any credit on screen.

Boucher had managed to complete the script for this final episode, 'Star One', around Christmas time. One thing was clear from the storyline and that was that both script editor and producer had agreed that Travis had now run out of potential, and this story was to be the vehicle for building up to his death in a spectacular fashion in a confrontation that would leave Blake nearly dead as well. However, Blake's other arch rival, Servalan, would be given a more uncertain fate, with questions left unanswered over what exactly happened to her, so that the character could easily be brought back if the series was given the green light for a third season.

Maloney started location work in a disused quarry in Cinderford, shooting from 5 to 7 February. He began taking the cast through rehearsals as soon as Martinus had finished work on 'The Keeper' and the final two-day studio session for the season commenced on 6 March. The next and final day dealt with the cliffhanger for the season and the death scene for Croucher, which was aptly the last sequence to be recorded that evening.

During editing, Maloney had to work fast to meet the 3 April broadcast date, and succeeded. 'Star One' is widely regarded as one of the best episodes the

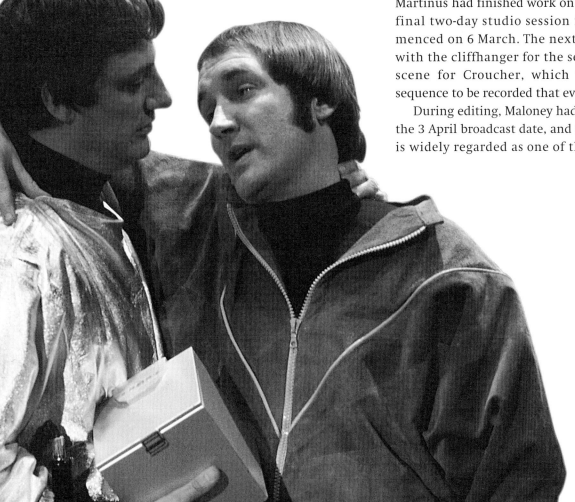

Paul Darrow as Avon and Michael Keating as a somewhat intoxicated Vila in 'Gambit'.

programme ever produced, and it was certainly one of the most watched that season. The ratings had hovered on the 7-8 million viewer mark throughout the run. There were none of the unexpected 10 million plus highs of the previous season, but the figures did prove that there was a steady following for the show. Most importantly, the regular ratings led to the decision to renew the series for a third and final season. At that stage, it seemed as though it would bring the whole series to a natural end, and let it go out while it was still popular. 'Star One' was watched by 8.2 million people. It seemed then to everyone concerned with the series that, if they were lucky, it would be back to normal in about four months with a new batch of stories to record. That, however, was not going to be the case.

Discussions between Boucher, Maloney and Terry Nation had resulted in the decision that Nation would top and tail the season, writing the resolution to the seemingly inescapable fate of the *Liberator* at the end of 'Star One', and bringing the season and series as a whole to its conclusion with the final episode. Nation would also have the option to write one, possibly two more episodes through the course of Season Three's run.

Michael Keating as Vila with Orac, whose voice was supplied initially by Derek Farr. The vocal duties were to be taken over by Peter Tuddenham.

As before, Boucher was already drafting in writers to start developing plot lines, with Robert Holmes commissioned and Allan Prior and Roger Parkes happy to return. Boucher himself was also working on some story ideas. As far as the directors were concerned, although he had missed out on 'Star One', Vere Lorrimer was certainly keen to return. The element left to be settled was the cast.

All of the actors had been with the show now for two years, appearing throughout, with the exception of David Jackson. Their contracts for a definite run of twenty-six episodes were now at an end, and salaries and availability inevitably had to be renegotiated for the next set of episodes. It was then that it became clear that both Gareth Thomas and Sally Knyvette wanted to leave. Paul Darrow, Michael Keating and Jan Chappell were happy to stay, but the series was about to lose Jenna, and more importantly, Blake's 7 was about to lose Blake!

The most obvious route to take with the narrative

Servalan gains control of the *Liberator* in 'The Harvest of Kairos'.

for the season would be to have the characters trying to regroup after the climcatic space battle at the end of Season Two, and finding that Blake and Jenna simply didn't survive, or just leave it so they never get back to the *Liberator*, which they had to abandon in the first place due to damage inflicted during the combat. It was certainly a problem, but one that had to be overcome. Thomas was not available for recording, having returned to working in the theatre for a season at the Royal Shakespeare Company, so no new material showing the fate of Blake could be made. As it would turn out, Thomas would not prove averse to making guest appearances in the series, but for the moment, that was not a possibili-

ty. Sally Knyvette, like David Jackson before her, was not happy with the development of her character, hence her decision to go.

New characters would have to be created to bring the crew of the *Liberator* back up to the title's designation of '7' crew members on board the ship. Once again, Maloney started casting, interviewing actors and actresses for the parts available, while Boucher drew up the new characters who would be brought into the series during the first couple of episodes for Season Three - a season that everyone was planning as the last. As had already been proved with *Blake's 7*, however, little ever seemed to run as smoothly as it was expected to!

The floor manager instructs the cast during rehearsals for 'The Keeper', with instructions being relayed to him through his headset by the director, Derek Martinus.

Bruce Purchase as Gola runs through a scene prior to its recording for broadcast.

In 'Gambit' the *Liberator's* crew enjoy the
liberal environment of Freedom City.

5 Season 2
Episode Guide

Season Two

Regular Cast Members

Blake – Gareth Thomas
Jenna – Sally Knyvette
Vila – Michael Keating
Avon – Paul Darrow
Gan (Stories B1-B5) – David Jackson
Cally – Jan Chappell
Voice of Zen and Orac – Peter Tuddenham
Servalan (Stories B3, B5-B6, B8, B10-B13) – Jacqueline Pearce
Travis (Stories B3, B5-B6, B8, B10-B13) – Brian Croucher

Regular Production Team

Producer – David Maloney
Script Editor – Chris Boucher

B1: Redemption
Written by Terry Nation.

Avon reasons that if they keep the *Liberator* out of the sector, shown in the background during Orac's visual prediction of the ship's destruction, the ship will never be blown up. That possibility is taken out of the crew's hands as the craft is drawn to a vast space station, failing to answer their commands to change course, and they encounter the race who created the *Liberator*, who happen to want it back.

Alta One – Sheila Ruskin
Alta Two – Harriet Philpin
Slave – Roy Evans
Director – Vere Lorrimer
Designer – Sally Hulke
Broadcast: 9 January 1979 1920-2010hrs

B2: Shadow
Written by Chris Boucher.

The *Liberator* heads for Space City, with Blake intent on buying the services of the mafia-like Terra Nostra to help him infiltrate Earth. Jenna has had past dealings with Largo, but instead of helping, he takes her prisoner with Blake and Avon, while Vila is elsewhere in the city's gambling centre enjoying the pleasures therein. On board the *Liberator*, Orac, who is now under alien control, begins to terrorize Cally with his newfound powers.

Largo – Derek Smith
Hanna – Adrienne Burgess
Bek – Karl Howman
Chairman – Vernon Dobtcheff
Enforcer – Archie Tew
Director – Jonathan Wright-Miller
Designer – Paul Allen
Broadcast: 16 January 1979 1915-2010hrs

Derek Smith as Largo on the set of
'Shadow'.

B3: Weapon
Written by Chris Boucher.

A technician called Coser, working for the
Federation, has developed an invention called
Imipak, a weapon which can be fired at people with
no visible effect, until a key is pressed which will
then kill them days, or even years later, over any dis-
tance. Servalan uses a clone Blake to get the device
off Coser, and all of the crew of the *Liberator* are
shot by Travis and allowed to escape, as she knows
that no matter where they are, when she presses the
key . . .

Coser – John Bennett
Fen – Kathleen Byron
Carnell – Scott Fredericks
Rashel – Candace Glendenning
Officer – Graham Simpson
Director – George Spenton-Foster
Designer – Mike Porter
Broadcast: 23 January 1979 1915-2010hrs

B4: Horizon
Written by Allan Prior.

Moving to a distant point in the galaxy to avoid
Federation ships, the *Liberator* comes across just
that, as they detect a freighter heading for a world
called Horizon, which is practically unknown to
Zen. This, and the fact that the Federation sends a
freighter there once a year, intrigues Blake, who
teleports down with all his crew, except for Avon. As
Blake, Jenna, Vila and Gan are captured and put into
slavery, Avon contemplates the possibility of pilot-
ing the *Liberator* solo, and whether he'd survive on
his own.

Kommissar – William Squire
Assistant Kommissar – Brian Miller
Ro – Dariell Angadi
Selma – Souad Faress
Chief Guard – Paul Haley
Director – Jonathan Wright-Miller
Designer – Paul Allen

Krantor's lair in 'Gambit'.

B5: Pressure Point
Written by Terry Nation.

Blake takes the *Liberator* back to Earth, and tells the crew that he intends to destroy Control, the centre of the Federation's computer network, with the assistance of Kasabi and her rebels, but she has been captured by Servalan and Travis. They use Kasabi's daughter, Veron, to try and capture Blake, but he manages to get to Control. All is not what it appears, and it will take an act of supreme sacrifice by Gan for Blake and the others to get out alive.

Kasabi – Jane Sherwin
Veron – Yolande Palfrey
Arle – Alan Halley
Berg – Martin Conner
Mutoid – Sue Bishop
Director – George Spenton-Foster
Designer – Mike Porter
Broadcast: 6 February 1979 2010-2100hrs

B6: Trial
Written by Chris Boucher

Travis is on trial, framed by Servalan so he will be unable to provide any evidence over her inability to capture Blake. Wracked with guilt over Gan's death, Blake seeks solitude on a desolate planet's surface, where he befriends Zil, a parasitic lifeform, who is absorbed by the planet. Now over his grief, Blake leads an attack on the Federation's Space Command, unwittingly providing Travis with the chance he needs to escape as he's pronounced guilty on board.

Samor – John Savident
Bercol – John Bryans
Rontane – Peter Miles
Thania – Victoria Fairbrother
Zil – Claire Lewis
Par – Kevin Lloyd
Lye – Graham Sinclair
Guard Commander – Colin Dunn
Director – Derek Martinus
Designer – Gerry Scott
Broadcast: 13 February 1979 1915-2010hrs

B7: Killer

Written by Robert Holmes.

On the planet Fosforan, Avon and Vila try to negoti-
ate with Tynus for a T-P Crystal, vital for Blake to be
able to crack Federation codes, with Avon calling in
an old debt from him. Blake, meanwhile, monitors
the salvage operation on an ancient vessel, and Cally
senses something is wrong, so he teleports down to
witness the autopsy on a body found on board. The
body momentarily comes to life, and unleashes a
lethal plague.

Bellfriar – Paul Daneman
Gambrill – Colin Farrell
Tynus – Ronald Lacey
Tak – Colin Higgins
Bax – Michael Gaunt
Wiler – Morris Barry
Director – Vere Lorrimer
Designer – Sally Hulke
Broadcast: 20 February 1979 1920-2010hrs

B8: Hostage

Written by Allan Prior.

In the aftermath of an intense Federation attack on
the *Liberator*, Blake receives a message from Travis,
who suggests a meeting on the planet Exbar, saying
that as they are both now outlaws, they should pool
their resources. As further incentive for Blake to go,
Travis reveals that he is holding Blake's cousin, Inga,
as a hostage and that he'll kill her if Blake does not
come. Blake, Avon and Vila are captured on the planet surface, and with Servalan on her way, they have
to find a way to get back to the *Liberator*.

Ushton – John Abineri
Inga – Judy Buxton
Joban – Kevin Stoney
Molok – James Coyle
Space Commander – Andrew Robertson
Mutoid – Judith Porter
Director – Vere Lorrimer
Designers – Gerry Scott and Steve Brownsey
Broadcast: 27 February 1979 1915-2010hrs

Deep Roy as Klute at Space City's gambling
centre, The Big Wheel, in 'Gambit'.

Blake's 7

Jacqueline Pearce as Servalan in her quarters during a recording break whilst making 'Gambit'.

B9: Countdown
Written by Terry Nation.

The Federation are holding the population of the planet Albian at bay, stopping revolution with the threat of detonating a solium radiation device, which would wipe out all humanoid life, but leave all of the buildings intact. The *Liberator* crew arrive after the inevitable revolution has taken place and the device has been activated, but the detonation device, so Orac declares, is within one of Albian's polar caps. Avon has to teleport there and work alongside an old enemy, Grant, to try and stop it. Blake finds out that the Federation Central Control is at a place called Star One, and that only a cyber surgeon called Docholli knows its location.

Grant – Tom Chadbon
Provine – Paul Shelley
Cauder – James Kerry
Ralli – Lindy Alexander
Selson – Robert Arnold
Tronos – Geoffrey Snell
Vetnor – Sidney Kean
Arrian – Nigel Gregory
Director – Vere Lorrimer
Designers – Gerry Scott and Steve Brownsey
Broadcast: 6 March 1979 1915-2010hrs

B10: Voice from the Past
Written by Roger Parkes.

Under the influence of a telepathic message, Blake abandons plans for the crew to rest from their search for Star One, and forces them to go to the desolate asteroid P-K 118. There he finds the guerilla leader Shivan, heavily bandaged from severe injuries, and a former Federation official, Ven Glynd, who propose to join forces with him to try and denounce the Federation at a summit meeting on the planet Atlay . . . But, Shivan is actually Travis under heavy disguise, and Avon and Cally have to race to try and break the telepathic hold over Blake as the others teleport down to Atlay leaving them with Shivan on the *Liberator* . . .

Governor Le Grand – Frieda Knorr
Ven Glynd – Richard Bebb
Nagu – Martin Read
Director – George Spenton-Foster
Designer – Ken Ledsham
Broadcast: 13 March 1979 1920-2010hrs

B11: Gambit
Written by Robert Holmes.

The *Liberator* arrives at Freedom City. Blake, Jenna and Cally teleport down to search for Docholli, unaware that both Travis and Servalan have second-guessed him, and are both waiting there, certain that Blake would eventually turn up to look for the cyber-surgeon. Avon and Vila, meanwhile, manage to reduce Orac in size, and take him with them to Freedom City's gambling centre, The Big Wheel, where they use him to help beat the gambling machines. Eventually, Docholli reveals that he does not know the location of Star One at all, but that another surgeon called Lurgen does have that information. The search continues . . .

Krantor – Aubrey Woods
Docholli – Denis Carey
Chenie – Nicolette Roeg
Cevedic – Paul Grist
Toise – John Leeson
Jarriere – Harry Jones
Zee – Michael Halsey
Croupier – Sylvia Coleridge
Klute – Deep Roy
Director – George Spenton-Foster
Designer – Ken Ledsham
Broadcast: 20 March 1979 1920-2010hrs

Darrow, Keating and Aubrey Woods as Krantor rehearsing for their scenes together in 'Gambit'.

Avon and Vila conquer the Big Wheel
using Orac to help them win at
gambling in 'Gambit'.

B12: The Keeper
Written by Allan Prior.

Lurgen's brain print, containing the information Blake needs, is on an amulet worn by members of the Royal Family of the planet Goth, which the *Liberator* arrives at. Distracted by a chance to attack and destroy Travis's ship, Avon leaves Vila, Jenna and Blake stranded on Goth, where they are attacked, with only Blake getting back to the *Liberator* on its return. Travis, who survived Avon's attack, beats them to the brain point, but due to an implant in the most unlikely of heads, which relays the data on hearing a certain phrase, Blake gains Star One's location as well, and sets off after Travis.

Gola – Bruce Purchase
Tara – Freda Jackson
Rod – Shaun Curry
Fool – Cengiz Saner
Old Man – Arthur Hewlett
Patrol Leader – Ron Tarr
Director – Derek Martinus
Designer – Eric Walmsley
Broadcast: 27 March 1979 1915-2010hrs

B13: Star One
Written by Chris Boucher.

Star One is breaking down, Servalan has found out that all the technicians who remained on the planet to service the system have been taken over by aliens from Andromeda, to pave the way for a galactic invasion. The *Liberator* crew find Star One controls a vast anti-matter minefield, which Travis is helping to close down to let the invasion begin. He has effectively betrayed mankind. In a confrontation, Travis wounds Blake severely, before Avon kills him and gets Blake back to the *Liberator* as the invasion force arrives.

Season Cliffhanger
Avon prepares to face the invasion force head on with the *Liberator*.

Lurena – Jenny Twigge
Stot – David Webb
Parton – Gareth Armstrong
Durkim – John Brown
Leeth – Michael Maynard
Director – (Uncredited) David Maloney
Designer – Ken Ledsham and Ray London
Broadcast: 3 April 1979 1920-2010hrs

On the departure of Blake, Steven Pacey joined *Blake's 7* as Tarrant whilst Avon was pushed forward as the group's leader.

6 *Departures and Arrivals*

Various ideas were tossed around as the production team attempted to come up with a satisfactory route to follow, now that it was clear that two of the principal characters were gone. Suggestions ranged from using the battle at the end of Season Two as an ideal way to blow the *Liberator* up and have the crew search for another ship, or just have them carry on but with a new character, who would ultimately be revealed at the season's conclusion as a Federation spy.

Eventually it was decided to push Avon forward to fill the leadership role vacated by Blake, and bring on board a new male character, who would go out of his way to antagonize Avon and prove his own worth as a more suitable leader for the crew. A second new character - a female with an alarming degree of expertise in weaponry - would bring the *Liberator's* humanoid quota back up to five.

The part of Tarrant was awarded to Steven Pacey, who had been acting since he was a child. This meant that a slightly different approach had to be adopted, as the part had been written for someone approaching their mid-thirties, compared to Pacey who was in his early twenties. The part of Dayna went to Josette Simon, who was still at Drama School when she was offered the role. She was spotted at TV Centre on a visit to a studio set with some other students, after which she was asked to audition and was chosen over such competition as

Marina Sirtis, who would later go on to find fame in a science fiction series as Troi in *Star Trek - The Next Generation.*

Apart from that, Darrow, Keating and Chappell signed up for the new run of thirteen episodes, as did Jacqueline Pearce, with Servalan making a total of nine appearances through the course of the season. Maloney and Boucher were there, as normal, but a new team of directors had to be appointed, with Vere Lorrimer, the only one signed up so far, agreeing to handle four episodes altogether.

The season would once again follow the pattern that had successfully been put into operation in Season Two, splitting the stories into two recording blocks of six and then seven episodes. Again, the location work would be carried out for all the stories in each block prior to any studio recording.

To even out the episode allocation, so that each director could be assigned two stories each, Maloney decided to direct one himself, leaving eight scripts to be allocated. Veteran BBC director Gerald Blake, who had just finished a tortuous experience making the hit *Doctor Who* story 'The Invasion of Time', agreed to handle two episodes, while Fiona Cumming, the first female director to work on the series, agreed to take on another two. The team was finalized by signing up Andrew Morgan and Desmond McCarthy with two episodes each, so now preproduction could start, approximately four

Josette Simon as Dayna who, like Pacey, joined *Blake's 7* as one of the regular cast from the beginning of Season 3 onwards.

months after 'Star One' had finished recording. Maloney decided to go first with 'Powerplay', the second half of a two-part story to start the season and bring the main characters back together on board the *Liberator*. The script was by Terry Nation.

For the first few episodes the location filming was centralized and based around Yorkshire, which offered a considerable variety of landscapes, ranging from scrublands to lush forests complete with waterfalls, that was ideal for the programme. Michael Keating was the first of the main cast to be called, and Maloney started the cameras rolling during the last week in July in the How Steen Gorge in North Yorkshire.

McCarthy was next, with material shot around the Ripon area for 'Volcano', which had been scripted by Allan Prior. Only a few days' work was needed from 3 August onwards. Lorrimer, meanwhile, was planning out the scenes he would need for two episodes that he'd scheduled to work on back to back; Nation's season opener, 'Aftermath', would require extensive beach sequences, while Boucher's 'City at the Edge of the World' had to have a wasteland area.

A suitable stretch of shoreline was found in Northumbria, near Bamburgh, and four days of shooting was successfully carried out during 7-10 August, with numerous stuntmen present for the extensive action shots that had to be done. The camera crew then moved back into the heart of North Yorkshire, to Pateley Bridge, and spent three days in horrendous weather conditions trying to finish off exterior scenes for Boucher's storyline. McCarthy and Lorrimer now returned to London, and Andrew Morgan arrived to start work around the grounds of the Leeds Polytechnic buildings on Roger Parkes's 'Children of Auron' during the following week.

By 27 August the entire unit went back to London, after nearly a month working in the North. The final script of the first block of six episodes, James Follett's 'Dawn of the Gods', only needed some of its scenes to be staged at the Ealing film studios, so Desmond McCarthy worked on them there from 28 to 30 August. Work could now begin on completing the studio footage that was required for 'Powerplay' and 'Aftermath' with Maloney and Lorrimer carrying out a few insert sequences, before rehearsals began in the first week of September.

As with the location filming, Maloney opted to go first, and started work in TV Centre on 'Powerplay'

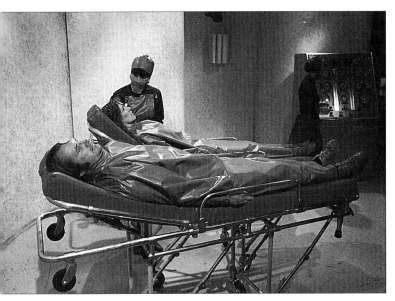

Keating and Chappell lie back, not for reasons of relaxation – they are about to become donors for spare part surgery in 'Powerplay'.

studio recording on 'Children of Auron', taking just two days from 23 to 24 October, but, like 'Volcano' and 'Aftermath', there were still some *Liberator* sequences that had to be completed. This opportunity came when McCarthy started recording 'Dawn of the Gods' in the first week of November, with the first of the three-day set-up being spent on the *Liberator* flight deck on all the noted stories, before McCarthy concentrated solely on his second story until 3 November.

During the rest of November the cast moved around from location to location, with material being recorded for five more stories. So far, the running order for the first four stories was 'Aftermath', 'Powerplay', 'Volcano', and then 'Dawn of the Gods'. 'City at the Edge of the World' and 'Children of Auron', although complete, would be moved to episodes six and seven in the actual broadcast order just prior to transmission.

for two days, 11-12 September. As before, the *Liberator* scenes remained untaped, due to the amount of studio space that the sheer bulk of the set required. Those scenes would have to wait until McCarthy's first script went before the cameras, with 'Volcano' being moved in and finished between 20 and 22 September. Maloney took the opportunity to shoot the scenes he needed on the *Liberator* bridge for 'Powerplay' during the first day, so Season Three's second episode was actually the first to be edited and dubbed, with the director for that episode returning to his producing duties from then onwards.

Lorrimer now concentrated on completing 'Aftermath' and 'City at the Edge of the World' throughout the course of October, with 'Aftermath' moving into studio during 2-3 October. Several scenes for Lorrimer's second story were staged in the same studio session on the 3 October. The same had been the case while the location shooting was being carried out, with scenes involving Cy Grant's character of Hal Mellanby in 'Aftermath' being done while 'City at the Edge of the World' was being shot in Ripon, due to the actor being unavailable for the earlier dates.

The future Doctor Who Colin Baker recorded his scenes for 'City' while that story moved in to TV Centre, with a three-day recording period from 11 to 13 October. Ten days later, Andrew Morgan started

Micheal Keating as Vila, pictured here in rehearsals for 'City At The Edge Of The World'.

With editing complete on the first two stories, Lorrimer was now able to start preproduction on his next two adventures, and Cumming and Blake now moved in to join the production team as well. Blake went first, taking the main cast down to Bovingdon aerodrome, which was practically abandoned and ideal for the script requirements of Ben Steed's 'The Harvest of Kairos'. Four days were spent there from 11 to 14 November.

At this location, problems continually arose with the main creature seen in this story. Described as a gigantic cocoon-weaving insect in the script, the finished result was a nightmare to operate, with the abdomen sac to the rear of the costume having in the end to be supported by an invisible wire, because the special effects man inside could not move the front of the costume with such weight bearing down on him. Many of the cast, of course, found this extremely amusing.

Lorrimer then began the relatively simple shoot that Trevor Hoyle's script of 'Ultraworld' required, moving into London and into the maze below Camden Town. The seemingly unending tunnels,

known as Camden Deep, have been used in countless films and television series, doubling up for everything from Soviet spy headquarters to, as in this case, alien spaceships. Lorrimer filmed from 19 to 20 November. On the following day, he took the cast for his next story, 'Moloch', by Ben Steed, to the ever-reliable Betchworth Quarry in Surrey, where three days between 21 and 23 November were spent on sequences for that episode.

Fiona Cumming was now ready to start on the location work for the first of her two instalments, with Boucher's script for 'Rumours of Death' requiring a stately home for scenes involving Servalan. After considering numerous possible sites, one was chosen in Oxford, where three days of shooting was staged from 26 November onwards. The second of her scripts, 'Sarcophagus', written by Tanith Lee, needed no location work as such, but did have two days of sequences that had to be staged at the Ealing Studios. One of the scenes from Lee's script required alien apparitions to be seen as part of a funeral procession, with each of the figures concealed behind masks. Later in the story it is revealed that these

Pacey as Tarrant and Simon as Dayna with a monster from 'The Harvest Of Kairos' that the production team nick-named, 'the nasty vacuum cleaner'.

The brisk pace of filming to tight
schedules meant relaxation periods
were critical to the actors.

Ronald Leigh-Hunt as C A One and
Beth Harris as C A Two in 'Children Of
Auron'.

apparitions are actually Avon, Vila and the rest of
the crew, so all five of the principal actors were
needed, and for once they were working out of character. Work on this material finished on 1 December
after which date the cast backtracked and started
rehearsals with Gerald Blake on the studio material
for 'The Harvest of Kairos'.

As stipulated in Steed's script, part of the story of
'The Harvest of Kairos' features the *Liberator* crew
stranded on the planet of the title, and having to
use an old Apollo moon shuttle to get back into
space and retake their ship. In an attempt to inject
some authenticity into these scenes, the designs for
the shuttle interior set were closely based on sketches taken from old newsreel of the 1969 moon land-
ings. Between 21 and 23 December, a day was spent
working on this set in cramped conditions, with the
second day concentrated on the scenes the story

needed featuring Servalan gaining control of the
Liberator flight deck. The decision was later taken to
slot in 'The Harvest of Kairos' as the fifth episode to
be broadcast. Luckily, the system of doing location
work prior to studio work had helped the show to
avoid being hit by a strike that nearly crippled TV
Centre's studios throughout November.

Following the traditional repeat run of the previous season's cliffhanger episode, 'Aftermath' was
screened on BBC1 on 7 January 1980, and exceeded
all expectations as far as ratings were concerned.
Following on from a clear dip in audience figures
during Season Two's run, the 'opening night' for
Season Three actually topped all of the episodes
from the previous year, with an incredible 9.5 million people tuning in. Throughout the ensuing
weeks, the ratings never dropped below the 8.8 million mark, and in the end, this fact would in part

A Mutoid on the set of 'Moloch'.

Opposite page: 'City At The Edge Of The World' featured a future Dr Who, a young Colin Baker as Bayban seen here with John J. Carney as Sherm.

change the anticipated future of the series.

Following a brief break for the cast over Christmas, studio work on the remaining six episodes that had to be completed would now basically run in broadcast order, with location work for all but the final two stories finished. As rehearsals for the studio sequences of 'Rumours of Death' began just after the new year, Terry Nation's draft for the final episode was being edited by Boucher. The end for *Blake's 7* was quite literally in sight.

Cumming finished her first episode across two days, 11-12 January, with rehearsals for Lee's 'Sarcophagus' starting after that. Set mainly on board the *Liberator*, with no additional cast required, Cumming used the three days allocated to her, from 21 to 23 January to shoot as well the inserts she needed on the *Liberator* bridge for 'Rumours of Death'.

Gerald Blake was already in preproduction on the penultimate story, 'Death-Watch', which Boucher had completed at very short notice, when it became clear that the script for this episode would need a great deal more work on it than time allowed. 'Death-Watch' had to be cheap, with a minimum of location work, and that basically involved two actors, plus Steven Pacey from the main cast, working around the derelict Wembley Exhibition Hall in London from 28 to 29 January. Even though the sequences in question were relatively brief, Blake took time to set up varying camera angles to make what little footage he had to shoot look good. Pacey doubled up as both Tarrant and that character's brother, Deeta.

After a couple of days spent running through the sections of 'Ultraworld' that had to be done in studio, the cast went before the cameras as February began, spending two days working with Lorrimer on the episode from 1 February onwards. As ever, the story was completed with the exception of all the *Liberator* flight deck scenes. As soon as shooting was over, Lorrimer started work on 'Moloch', which was actually part of a four-day studio session that ran from 10 to 13 February. The *Liberator* scenes for this episode and for 'Ultraworld' were staged on 10 February, followed by the main scenes for 'Moloch' from 11 February to the end of that recording session.

In between those two sessions, work on location for Nation's finale, called 'Terminal' had been carried out. In keeping with what now seemed almost

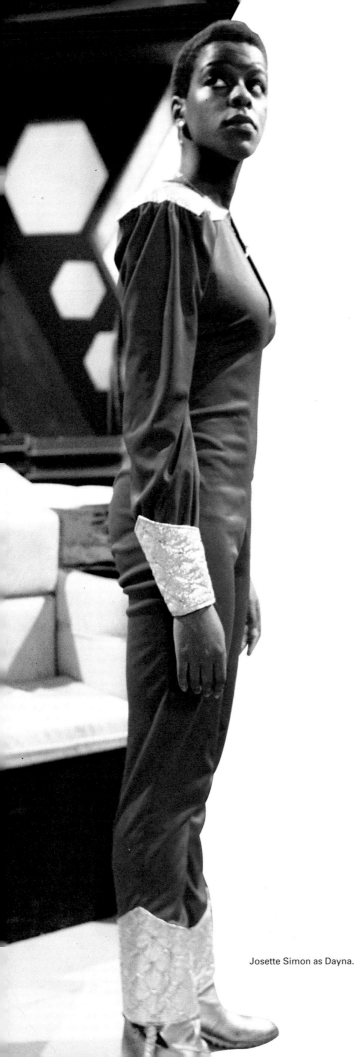

Josette Simon as Dayna.

to have become a tradition with the programme, the final episode of the season - and of what was anticipated to be the series as a whole - lost its director. 'Terminal' was due to be the second story of the year directed by Andrew Morgan, who had made 'Children of Auron', but dates overlapped with a war series he was working on elsewhere in the Drama Department. Maloney was therefore nearly forced to step in again, until Mary Ridge, a veteran drama director, accepted the assignment quite late in the day.

Three days in total were spent around the vast acreage surrounding Perton Hall in Oxford, with all the sequences involving the surface of the man-made planet Terminal being filmed. It was during that week that Maloney also managed to persuade Gareth Thomas to return as Blake, for a short scene towards the end of this story. Blake is seen in an illusion sequence induced in Avon's mind to make him believe Blake is alive on Terminal, but so badly wounded that he's unmoveable, which in turn allows Servalan to force Avon to give up the *Liberator* to her.

Thomas's scene revolved around his availability, and as he was still with the Royal Shakespeare Company, any trip to London for the day to record at TV Centre was out of the question. So a compromise was reached, and a set was rigged up at a local village hall, which the now bearded Thomas was able to commute to and from without missing a performance on stage. This was all done in the vicinity of Perton Hall, and only required Paul Darrow at the location for the morning it took to shoot the scene. Although the character of Blake was no longer supposedly real, he would still be seen in the series bearing his name as it came to its conclusion.

Back in London, Gerald Blake took the cast through the last few scenes he needed for 'Death-Watch', with the *Liberator* set used extensively during 21-23 February. The broadcast schedule was once more beginning to catch up with the production team, with 'Rumours of Death' being screened a couple of days after the penultimate studio session was wrapped.

Mary Ridge meanwhile began what were ostensibly the final rehearsals with the cast for 'Terminal'. Boucher and Nation had agreed when they were discussing the finale that it should be something quite spectacular, and the decision was made to engineer the total destruction of the *Liberator*, courtesy of a

Michael Keating as Vila during Season 3.

sections of the specially rigged set split open and rose up in the air, like the effects an earthquake has on a road surface, Tuddenham recorded the dying words of Zen as the computer finally faded away. And that was it. The party that followed went on into the small hours of the morning, and as soon as Ridge completed editing, a week or so prior to broadcast, the production office closed down.

It was then that the BBC made an extraordinary move. Maloney had moved on to the drama series *When the Boat Comes In*, taking over as its producer, and Boucher was due to move on as well, while the cast members were now actively seeking other work on either television or stage. The ratings were consistantly coming in at around the 9-9.5 million mark, with 'Moloch' even topping that with 10.4 million viewers. So, without anybody actually there to persuade them, the BBC management decreed that *Blake's 7* was sufficiently popular to warrant a fourth season. By then, however, it was literally too late to plan any episodes and start production up again in time to meet the series' annual January start date. It was also too late to bring back Maloney.

The first that many of the team behind the scenes or even the actors knew about the decision was when, as the end titles rolled up screen on 'Terminal' a voice stated that the series would be back the following year. Maloney was now under contract to his new series, but Boucher was still available, so a new producer had to be found. The most obvious choice, due to the sheer number of episodes he had directed over the past three seasons, was Vere Lorrimer, and he was happy to accept the offer when it was made to him.

As far as the cast were concerned, only Jan Chappell declined the chance to return. She had grown unhappy with some of the story lines over the last few episodes of Season Three, and felt that the programme was losing its way. Darrow, Keating, Pacey and Simon, on the other hand, quickly agreed to the contracts they were offered, as did Peter Tuddenham, who agreed to resume voicing Orac, with the promise of more work as the voice of the on-board computer for the new ship the crew would obviously have to obtain.

Blake's 7 had been given a reprieve that was not only unexpected, but was also totally unplanned for. Thirteen more adventures had to be made, and the production team had to start work on them from scratch.

cloud of particles in space that corrode the hull of the ship and then start rapidly to destroy its interior. Whatever the circumstances, these scenes would have to be be the last ones to be shot in studio, due to the complex nature of the effects that would be involved.

The 5 and 6 March were spent on all the other scenes for this final story, and 7 March marked the end for both the cast and crew. Ridge was a novice when it came to *Blake's 7*, as Maloney discovered at one point when she told him of her plans to have dozens of crew members crashing through the ceiling of the *Liberator's* bridge, as the corrosion took effect. Maloney then had to point out, much to her dismay, that there were only five humans on board at any one time.

On the evening of 7 March, the explosions began as Pearce's Servalan tried to fly the ship. Then, as the

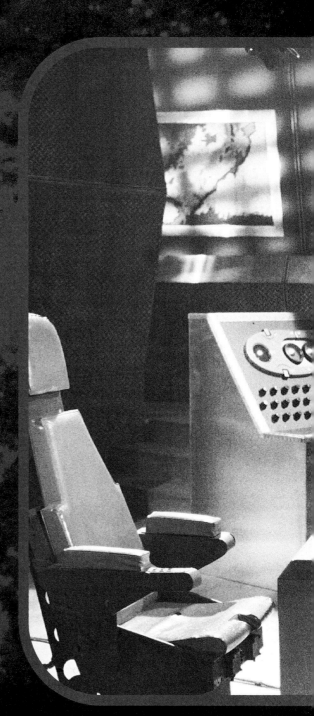

7 *Season 3*
Episode Guide

Season Three

Regular Cast Members
Avon – Paul Darrow
Vila – Michael Keating
Cally – Jan Chappell
Dayna – Josette Simon
Tarrant – Steven Pacey
Voice of Zen and Orac – Peter Tuddenham
Servalan (Stories C1-C3, C5, C7-C8, C11-C13) –
Jacqueline Pearce

Regular Production Team
Producer – David Maloney
Script Editor – Chris Boucher

C1: Aftermath
Written by Terry Nation.

The *Liberator* sustains heavy damage in the battle
with the ships from Andromeda, and Zen shuts the
life-support systems down, forcing the crew to abandon ship in life-pods. On the planet Sarran, Avon and
Orac are rescued from savage tribesmen by a young
woman called Dayna, and on the way back to her
base, they find Servalan stranded there as well.
Dayna's father, who adopted her, Hal Mellanby, is
killed by Servalan as she steals Orac, and Avon and
Dayna have to outwit the Sarran tribesmen before
returning to the *Liberator,* where they are confronted by a team of Federation guards.

Hal Mellanby – Cy Grant
Chel – Alan Lake
Lauren – Sally Harrison
Federation Trooper – Richard Franklin
Federation Trooper – Michael Melia
Director – Vere Lorrimer
Designers – Gerry Scott and Don Taylor
Broadcast: 7 January 1980 1915-2010hrs

Blake's 7

C2: Powerplay
Written by Terry Nation.

Stranded on the planet Chenga, Vila's wounds from his life-pod crash are treated by two primitives, who flee as a pair of Hitechs arrive and take Vila to their base to 'reintroduce him' to society. Cally and Servalan have been picked up by a hospital ship which is heading for Chenga. Avon and Dayna, meanwhile, are held captive by the Federation guards, but Captain Tarrant is revealed as an impostor who joins forces with them to regain control of the *Liberator*. Meanwhile, time is running out for Vila and Cally, as they find that if they're not rescued soon, they will literally end up as 'spare parts' for surgery on hospital ships.

Klegg – Michael Sheard
Lom – John Hollis
Harmon – Doyne Byrd
Mall – Michael Crane
Zee – Primi Townsend
Barr – Julia Vidler
Nurse – Catherine Chase
Receptionist – Helen Blatch
Director – (Uncredited) David Maloney
Designer – Gerry Scott
Broadcast: 14 January 1980 1915-2010hrs

C3: Volcano
Written by Allan Prior.

With Dayna and Tarrant now part of the crew of the *Liberator*, Avon seeks a base to work from on the planet Obsidian, but they are refused and betrayed by one of the people there, Bershar, who gives the location of the ship to Servalan's forces. Cally and Orac are captured and taken prisoner by Servalan, and it is up to Dayna and Tarrant to try and rescue them.

Hower – Michael Gough
Bershar – Malcolm Bullivant
Mori – Ben Howard
Battle Fleet Commander – Alan Bowerman
Milus – Russell Denton
Mutoid – Judy Matheson
Director – Desmond McCarthy
Designer – Gerry Scott
Broadcast: 21 January 1980 1915-2010hrs

C4: Dawn of the Gods
Written by James Follett.

Curious about what lies beyond the black hole the *Liberator* is heading for, Orac does not stop the ship spiralling through it, with the crew convinced they are about to die, but instead they land on an artificial world called Crandor. It is ruled by the Thaarn, a creature Cally remembers from the fairy tales of her childhood on Auron, who recognizes Cally's origins and decides to hold her captive to share in its loneliness. With the crew gone, it's up to Orac to stop the *Liberator* from being destroyed by the Thaarn's servants.

The Caliph – Sam Dastor
Groff – Terry Scully
The Thaarn – Marcus Powell
Director – Desmond McCarthy
Designers – Gerry Scott and Ray London
Broadcast: 28 January 1980 1915-2010hrs

C5: The Harvest of Kairos
Written by Ben Steed.

Jarvik, a construction worker with the Federation openly speaks of Servalan's incompetence in her attempts to capture the Liberator. He is brought before her, whereupon he tells her that he could do it with three ships. She agrees to let him. Tarrant leads an attempt to steal the Federation's freight of valuable kairopan from Kairos, and leads the *Liberator* straight into an elaborate ambush staged by Jarvik, a former Space Commander. Servalan now has the *Liberator*, and strands the crew on Kairos, with their only means of escape being an ancient NASA-like ship.

Jarvik – Andrew Burt
Dastor – Frank Gatliff
Shad – Anthony Gardner
Carlon – Sam Davies
Guard – Charles Jamieson
Director – Gerald Blake
Designer – Ken Ledsham
Broadcast: 4 February 1980 1915-2010hrs

C6: City at the Edge of the World
Written by Chris Boucher.

Tarrant is tricked into sending Vila down to the planet Keezam, where he is held by Bayban the Butcher, a flamboyant outlaw high on the Federation 'most wanted' list, who believes he has found the vault where all of Keezam's treasure is stored. Vila and Bayban's female accomplice, Kerril, find out that it is not a vault, but a matter transmitter. Avon and the rest of the *Liberator* crew teleport down to Keezam to try and rescue Vila, and confront Bayban and his men, but Vila and Kerril have been transported to a distant world, with seemingly no way of return.

Kerril – Carol Hawkins
Bayban – Colin Baker
Norl – Valentine Dyall
Sherm – John J. Carney
Director – Vere Lorrimer
Designers – Jerry Scott and Don Taylor
Broadcast: 11 February 1980 1915-2010hrs

C7: Children of Auron
Written by Roger Parkes.

Servalan captures an Auron pilot, infects him with a plague virus her scientists have created, and lets him head back to his planet where the disease runs riot. Cally is sent a telepathic message by her twin and the *Liberator* sets off to help her homeworld. It is all part of an elaborate scheme by Servalan to capture the *Liberator*, knowing that Cally would return to Auron in such a situation, and at the same time she plans to use the planet's cloning plant to breed an entire race in her likeness.

Franton – Sarah Atkinson
Deral – Rio Fanning
Ginka – Ric Young
C.A. One – Ronald Leigh-Hunt
C.A. Two – Beth Harris
Patar – Jack McKenzie
Pilot Four-Zero – Michael Troughton
Zelda – Jan Chappell
Director – Andrew Morgan
Designers – Gerry Scott and Ray London
Broadcast: 19 February 1980 1915-2010hrs

In 'The Harvest Of Kairos', Servalan tries a new scheme to try and capture the *Liberator*.

Blake's 7

C8: Rumours of Death
Written by Chris Boucher.

Avon allows himself to be captured returning to Earth, but it's part of a plan to trap a vicious Federation interrogator known as the Shrinker, who Avon believes was responsible for the death of his lover, Anna Grant. Both men are beamed on board the *Liberator*, and Avon discovers that Servalan is the real key to finding out the identity of Anna's killer, but that she is no longer exactly what could be termed as in control of the situation. Imprisoned in a dungeon under a mansion house on Earth, she is confronted by Avon, who discovers that a certain person might not be as dead as he thought.

Sula – Lorna Heilbron
Shrinker – John Bryans
Grenler – Donald Douglas
Chesku – Peter Clay
Forres – David Haig
Hob – David Gilles
Balon – Philip Bloomfield
Director – Fiona Cumming
Designers – Paul Munting and Ken Ledsham
Broadcast: 25 February 1980 1915-2010hrs

C9: Sarcophagus
Written by Tanith Lee.

A strange alien craft comes across the path of the *Liberator*, and Cally, Avon and Vila teleport on board. They find various artefacts laid out by a corpse, one of which Cally brings back to the ship with a ring before the alien tomb blows up. Via the artefact, an alien life form takes over Cally's body, and starts to stalk the *Liberator*, seeking to enslave the crew. With Zen and Orac seemingly dead, Avon has to confront the creature.

No guest cast (main cast played the apparitions)
Director – Fiona Cumming
Designer – Ken Ledsham
Broadcast: 3 March 1980 1915-2010hrs

C10: Ultraworld
Written by Trevor Hoyle.

Investigating an artificial planet, Cally is drawn to teleport on board. Avon, Tarrant and Dayna follow to rescue her, but find they are now in what is effectively a giant computer. The core of the planet is served by the Ultra, who wipe the brains of lifeforms they encounter and either feed them into the core or use them as drones. With Avon and Cally 'wiped', and Dayna and Tarrant held as part of an experiment for the Ultra to witness how humans breed, only Vila and Orac are left to try and free them. Surprisingly, this involves Orac using the riddles Vila has taught him in order to start confusing the core.

Ultras – Peter Richards, Ian Barritt, Stephen Jenn
Relf – Ronald Govey
Director – Vere Lorrimer
Designers – Jan Spoczynski and Ken Ledsham
Broadcast: 10 March 1980 1920-2010hrs

C11: Moloch
Written by Ben Steed.

The *Liberator* follows Servalan's ship to Sardos, which has a powerful generator capable of making the planet invisible. Tarrant and Vila beam on board a transporter to get on to the surface, with Avon and Dayna following later, once the teleport system is able to break through the barrier. A group of federation deserters have found technology that is able to duplicate any solid object, and after luring Servalan there, they intend to create a whole fleet using her ship as a blueprint. But the computer system they're using is far more than it appears.

Doran – David Harries
Grose – John Hartley
Lector – Mark Sheridan
Poola – Debbi Blythe
Chesil – Sabina Franklyn
Moloch – Deep Roy
Director – Vere Lorrimer
Designers – Jan Spoczynski and Ken Ledsham
Broadcast: 17 March 1980 1915-2010hrs

C12: Death-Watch
Written by Chris Boucher.

The outcome of a war between two planets is to be decided by man-to-man combat, with a contestant representing either side. The *Liberator* crew decide to watch, until they see that one of the contestants is Tarrant's brother, Deeta, who is killed. The crew immediately become suspicious of Servalan's involvement as a neutral arbiter, and suspect Deeta's opponant was in fact an android, which Tarrant then challenges.

Vinni – Mark Elliott
Max – Stewart Bevan
Karla – Katherine Iddon
Commentator – David Sibley
Director – Gerald Blake
Designer – Ken Ledsham
Broadcast: 24 March 1980 1915-2010hrs

C13: Terminal
Written by Terry Nation.

Following instructions being relayed to him, Avon takes control of the *Liberator* and heads for the artificial planet, Terminal, flying straight through a cloud of particles that start to corrode the hull of the vessel. In an underground centre, Avon is drugged and an illusion of meeting a badly injured Blake is induced - all part of an elaborate plan by Servalan to capture the *Liberator*.

Season Cliffhanger
(intended end of the series)
Servalan tries to escape as the *Liberator* disintegrates, and the crew are trapped on Terminal, with no apparant means of escape . . .

Blake – Gareth Thomas
Kostos – Gillian McCutcheon
Taron – Ri chard Clifford
Sphere Voice – David Healy
Links – Deep Roy, Gareth Milne, Stuart Fell
Director – Mary Ridge
Designer – Jim Clay
Broadcast: 31 March 1980 1915-2010hr

Josette Simon pictured at a press call marking the launch of Season 3.

Paul Darrow (pictured here) Michael Keating,
and Peter Tuddenham as the voice of Orac,
were the only original cast members to have
stayed with the series since Season One.

8 The Beginning of the End

One of the first people Vere Lorrimer turned to as he began drawing up plans for Season Four was Terry Nation, who was now living and working in America. But it soon became clear that Nation would not be available to write any of the thirteen new scripts that had to be commissioned. He was too busy, because like Maloney and Boucher before him, the last thing he had expected was for the series to continue.

Before any work on storylines could begin, Lorrimer had two problems to overcome. First, Jan Chappell had now stated that she would not be returning as Cally, but that was simple enough to solve. Another actress could be cast as a new character drafted in to join the crew. The second problem was not quite so easy to resolve, as it involved the principal characters' mode of transportation. Quite simply, there wasn't one. Nation had atomized the *Liberator* at the conclusion of 'Terminal', and its fate had been so definite and final that there was no acceptable or plausible way to bring it back. Something new was needed.

Boucher had mulled over the idea of giving Avon and the others a planetary base to operate from during Season Three, with 'Volcano' plot revolving specifically around their search for such a venue. He determined that the first two episodes would deal with this, and also provide a new vessel. The combined thinking of script editor, producer and series creator concluded that the new ship should be vulnerable. The *Liberator* had been too much of a 'supercraft'. This time, if the crew required teleport systems, or wanted to improve the power of their engines, they would have to search out whatever it was that was needed to achieve this. To this end, a battered mining ship called the *Scorpio* was created, and one of the first things that the designers were told when it came to planning out the set was to ensure that it was nowhere near as bulky as the *Liberator* flight deck. Three years of scheduling nightmares had taught Lorrimer to avoid things like that.

Boucher started working on the first three episodes, with each one centring around bringing together the elements that would be needed to give the crew the mobility they had lost since the destruction of their old ship. The first episode would deal with the acquisition of the *Scorpio* and a base; the second instalment concerned their efforts to find the power to create a teleport system; and the third story told of their quest to find some way of augmenting the engines of the *Scorpio* so that they would be able to outrun any Federation starships.

To this end, Boucher gave himself the task of writing the season's opening story, as he was simply the best man to re-establish the characters with the viewers after their lengthy absence on screen between Seasons Three and Four. Ben Steed would then handle the second story, while James Follett tackled the third. Other writers from the 'old guard' were now beginning to return to the fold - Robert Holmes, Allan Prior, Roger Parkes and Tanith Lee - all of whom quickly started working on new story lines.

There was some doubt for a time as to whether Servalan would be brought back, with a new character of equally malicious qualities being devised called Sleer, but when Jacqueline Pearce reiterated that she was happy to return, Sleer simply became an alias for Servalan, with the character now in hiding but still maintaining her lust for power. This gave Boucher and the writers the added opportunity of having her kill anyone she came across who happened to recognize her from her past.

Although it cannot be denied that stylistically Lorrimer brought a different feel to the series when he took over, he maintained the recording process that had been established by Maloney over the first three years, namely, dividing the episodes into two distinct batches, and then completing all the location work before moving into the studio for each batch. One minor change that was introduced was to have all the episodes with one-word titles: thus the first three episodes ran as 'Rescue', 'Power' and 'Stardive'. By the beginning of 1981, Roger Parkes had completed work on 'Headhunter', so preproduction could at least begin on the first few stories.

One of the first directors Lorrimer approached, when news came through of the series' rebirth, was Mary Ridge. His main idea was that she could carry on where she left off with 'Terminal' and oversee the direct sequel with 'Rescue'. Out of the first block of six episodes, she agreed to direct four in total, with an option to work also on the second block at a later stage if she wanted to. The two remaining stories were assigned to a director new to the show; Lorrimer was familiar with the previous work of David Sullivan-Proudfoot and liked his style, and so it was he who started to draw up filming schedules with Ridge.

Sullivan-Proudfoot had also expressed his willingness to stay with the series beyond the first batch of episodes, so Lorrimer tentatively sounded out another director new to *Blake's 7*, Brian Lighthill, and Season Two veteran Gerald Blake, both of whom said they would be available from June onwards to join the production team. One advantage that soon became apparent was that there was some leeway in

Glynis Barber as Soolin, strikes a dramatic pose at her press call where she was introduced as the latest member of the cast.

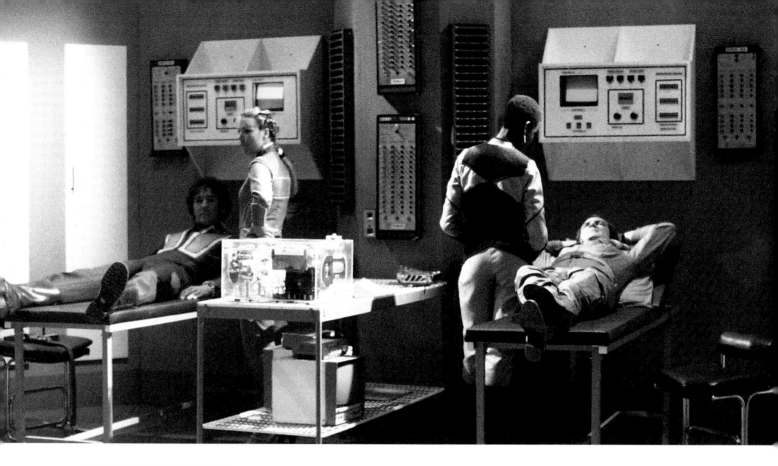

Barber and Simon during the first
recording block for Season 4.

the production timing compared with the tight schedules Maloney had had to contend with. Lorrimer basically had eight months to complete the season, in comparison with the previous standard of five to six months. The BBC had declared that it wanted *Blake's 7* to return as part of the 1981 autumn line-up, so 'Rescue' would be needed for screening at some point during September.

Casting began for the new crew member, who had been given the name of Soolin, and Lorrimer offered the role to Glynis Barber. In fact, she had previous experience on the show, having been given her first television acting work by Michael E. Briant in Season One's 'Project Avalon', in which she had been cast as the lead Mutoid. In similar situations - say, for example, when a new *Doctor Who* companion joins the cast of that programme - actors have to go through a period of being accepted by the regular cast members, and in some instances this can be awkward if the cast have got on particularly well with the original actor, and therefore resent the new arrival. Barber had no such problems, as she already knew the long-standing cast members of *Blake's 7* with Darrow and Keating have appeared in

her previous story.

The only other new member of the cast came about as a result of the promise made to Peter Tuddenham to give him a computer voice part in addition to that of Orac. Thus Slave, a subservient and humble machine, was created and given to Tuddenham to bring to life vocally as the *Scorpio's* on-board computer.

Rehearsals began on 15 February, Ridge and the cast returned to Perton Hall in Oxford, with the sets for the entrance to the underground base in 'Terminal' being brought out of storage to recreate the setting for Season Three's finale. Two days, 23-24 February, were spent filming at Perton. With only a day in between shoots, Ridge then assembled the cast at Betchworth Quarry from 26 to 28 February, where the material that had been rehearsed for the exterior scenes of 'Power' was filmed.

Unusually, rather than let Sullivan-Proudfoot move in to film his material, Ridge continued straight on and started the cameras rolling on location for her next two episodes out of the first batch. Six days were spent in concentrated filming around the Dorking area of Surrey, with three days from 3 to 5 March confined to a forest area and close to a wrought-iron bridge on Box Hill filming 'Headhunter'. After that, 6-8 March saw the team located in a nearby quarry, with a return to Betchworth being ruled out logistically. This material was for 'Animals', Allan Prior's only script for the season, and, as with 'Headhunter', the atrocious weather and continuous rain made filming near impossible. Props failed to work, actors slid about in the thick mud and soaking grass, and the camera lens continually misted up, but nevertheless, only 'Animals' really suffered, with one or two scenes later having to be restaged in TV Centre's studios.

Prior's script was actually drafted with Cally in mind as the main character to be featured from the regular cast, but due to Chappell's decision to leave, the script was quickly rewritten for Dayna to inherit the plot line. Chappell did, however, return briefly to record a voiceover for the opening scenes of 'Rescue', so that it could be firmly established that Cally had been killed in the explosions in the underground laboratories on the planet Terminal.

David Sullivan-Proudfoot started work on 'Stardrive' shortly after Ridge had finished, taking the main cast to Dunstable in Bedfordshire, where a quarry was used for three days from 11 to 13 March. Because of the elaborate vehicle stunts that were due to be staged in this episode, the director actually went to the site two days before filming began and carefully planned out the camera positioning for each shot, so that accidents with moving objects hitting valuable equipment could be avoided. Sullivan-Proudfoot stayed on site with a single camera operator for one or two days after the cast left in order to complete some insert shots for the various chase sequences 'Stardrive' needed.

Several cast members rejoined Ridge for the next few days, with various sections of both 'Rescue' and 'Headhunter' being shot at the Ealing film studios between 15 and 19 March, while at the same time planning and rehearsing began on 'Traitor', Robert Holmes's first script for the season, which Sullivan-Proudfoot was due to direct.

A vast quarry in Dorset a few miles from Wareham had been selected by Sullivan-Proudfoot, and three days' work was carried out around that area during 21-23 March.. Apart from the various model sequences the stories needed, the first stage

Damien Thomas as Atlan, leader of the Space Rats in 'Stardrive'.

Dicken Ashworth as Gunn Sar battles
with Paul Darrow in 'Power'.

of working on the first recording block was now over.

Operations now moved back to TV Centre for the three-month period from April to June. At about this it became clear that the BBC would not be requiring a fifth season. The fourth season was definitely going to be the last. Lorrimer and Boucher agreed that it would be good if they could devise a way to go out on a high, and even if possible top the spectacular nature of 'Terminal's last few scenes. Boucher had an idea, but it all hinged on the willingness to participate of a certain actor.

By the second week of April, Ridge was ready to take 'Rescue' before the cameras, and so between 10 and 11 April, the regular cast acclimatized themselves to the interior set of the *Scorpio* flight deck, which would play such a prominent part in their work for the next few months. The same basic sets were reused for the next studio session, which came just over ten days later as Ridge started work on 'Power' from 23 to 25 April. Sullivan-Proudfoot took up a certain amount of the three-day period on 24 April, as he completed the sequences he needed for 'Stardrive' on the *Scorpio* bridge set, and while Ridge started editing the first two stories, he began rehearsing for the middle two of the first six episodes due to be broadcast.

With 'Stardrive's ship scenes complete, the rest of the material, mainly involving the 'Space Rats' headquarters, was recorded over two days in studio from

In 'Assassin' the crew are victims of a
double-cross and the true identity of
dancer Piri is revealed.

8 to 9 May. Sullivan-Proudfoot promptly started
rehearsing for 'Traitor', which moved to TV Centre
just under two weeks later, from 22 and 24 May.
Only Ridge's final two stories from the first recording block now remained unfinished, and for this
season, the location filming for the next block did
not overlap with the studio work for the first batch.
'Headhunter' was first, with two days at the end of
the first week of June spent working on the script.

Some sequences of 'Headhunter' remained
incomplete and were carried over to the next three-
day studio session, 18-20 June, which mainly concentrated on 'Animals'. The first and last days of the
period included some work on 'Headhunter', with
only Lynda Bellingham from that story's guest cast
being needed with the regulars for both sessions.All
the sequences on the *Scorpio* for both episodes were
staged on the last day.

With stories one to six 'in the can', the preproduction work on the second batch of episodes started. During the recording of Season Three, a success-
ful exercise in location filming had been to work on
several stories in one main area over a couple of
weeks - in that instance, North Yorkshire. Lorrimer
decided to try the same system, with two weeks

scheduled for filming around Dorset.

Once again, however, the 'lost director' scenario
arose, with Gerald Blake having to back out of working on both Bill Lyons' script for 'Games' and Tanith
Lee's 'Sand'. Lorrimer sought a replacement at very
short notice, and this time chose to give Vivienne
Cozens her chance at directing mainstream television drama for the first time. Up until that time, she
had worked as a production assistant on numerous
programmes at the BBC, including *Blake's 7* so
unlike Ridge the year before, she was no novice
when it came to understanding the mechanics of
the series. The other director signed up by Lorrimer
at that point was Brian Lighthill, who was assigned
the tenth and eleventh episodes, with scripts by
Colin Davies for 'Gold' and Robert Holmes for
'Orbit'.

Lighthill would share the Dorset trip with Cozens
and David Sullivan-Proudfoot, who was back to
direct his third and final script for the season,
'Assassin', by Rod Beacham. As things turned out, it
would be an eventful trip.

Cozens was the first to start filming, with
'Games'. Three days were spent shooting around a
quarry near Swanage, working from 6 to 8 July. As

soon as this was over, the cast moved to join Lighthill at a refuse centre in Poole, where initial scenes for 'Gold' were shot during 9-10 July, before moving on to a nearby quarry from 11 to 12 July. It was during these four days that Lorrimer had to cope with an emergency.

Sullivan-Proudfoot had been taken seriously ill, and was basically out of the running as far as filming in Dorset was concerned. There was no time to hire a replacement, or to reschedule as the cast and costumes had arrived from London. Unlike Maloney, Lorrimer had chosen to stay firmly in the producer's seat during his run on the series, but now, with no alternatives left, he stepped behind the cameras for the only time that year. Proudfoot had completed his camera scripts and recording schedules, so Lorrimer used them as the basis for the five days spent around Bovington from 13 to 17 July, after

which everybody returned to London.

Before any studio work began, Cozens went to the Ealing studios, and worked for five days on the complex on-camera effects that were needed for 'Sand'. This episode had the cast working in an environment that one or two have since described as 'Like walking through a dust storm'. Rehearsals were now due to start for the studio footage.

Plans were also coming together for the last episode, with a finale that Boucher had completed the script for. Gareth Thomas, in a move to rid himself of a problem he had been facing since he left the programme – namely, that as the series was still going and bore his character's name in the title, directors of other programmes assumed that he would be unavailable for work - had agreed to return for the last episode on one condition: Blake had to be killed off on screen, and with enough

The late Roy Kinnear appeared as Keiller an old, but distrustful acquaintence of Avon in 'Gold'

blood to show categorically that he was dead, thus leaving the actor unquestionably available for other work. Few had seen the script in progress, and it was actually kept under wraps until the last possible moment.

As Sullivan-Proudfoot, fit and well again, returned to start studio work on 'Assassin', the cast were oblivious of the eventual fate that all their characters would face. The seventh story due to be broadcast was finished over three days, 13-15 August, including extensive work on the *Scorpio* set. The season's start date had now been scheduled as 28 September, so time was once more beginning to catch up with the production team. The location filming for the final two episodes had not been done, and a director had yet to be signed up for the penultimate episode, as Lorrimer's request to Gerald Blake had again met with 'Sorry, not available'.

Vivienne Cozens was next into TV Centre, and shot the studio footage for her stories back to back. The episodes were taken in reverse order: 'Sand' came first on 28-29 August with 'Games' following on 10-12 September. In between, Viktors Ritelis, who had been recruited to direct Simon Masters' script for episode twelve, 'Warlord', shot for two days back at Betchworth Quarry, from 31 August to 1 September, before spending a day and a half at the Friary Shopping Centre in Guildford from 2 to 3 September. The second day was noted as finishing early to allow the actors to leave before shoppers flooded the area when the schools emptied for the day.

'Gold' came next at TV Centre, and Lighthill had all of the scenes finished by 26 September, after a two-day recording period. From 27 September onwards, intensive rehearsals began for 'Orbit', which was a well-scripted vehicle for Avon and Vila. It marked the only time in the programme's history that no location work or sequences at Ealing had to be carried out, with the episode being effectively 'studio bound'. Lighthill completed it in three days between 9 and 11 October.

The next day, 12 October, Mary Ridge, started filming around an area of woodland in Camberley, in the heart of Surrey, on the final story of all, which had the simple title of 'Blake'. Battle weary, and with a livid scar across his face, Thomas was back with Darrow and Keating once again, and three days were spent on site, finishing all the exterior scenes the story needed by 15 October.

Just under a week later, Ritelis recorded the studio sessions for 'Warlord' over three days from 22 to 24 October and Jacqueline Pearce made her final appearance as Servalan. She was not required for recording on 'Blake', as the character did not feature in the plot. The actress felt this was a personal snub to her, and has made her feelings quite clear on this matter in interviews in the past. From the viewpoint of the production team, they all felt that the audience would be expecting Servalan to move into shot in the final moments of 'Blake', and they wanted to avoid being that obvious, so she simply did not appear at all. The internal politics and arguments behind the scenes on any television series are as complex as they are contrived, and the true reasons for Servalan's omission from the final episode will probably never be known.

The final three days of filming took place in the first week of November, the second day being spent recording what has perhaps caused more arguments among followers of the series than anything else. Here Ridge staged the scenes for the last few frames of the episode and indeed the series. After Avon had killed Blake, all the main characters are fired upon by Federation guards and collapse one by one to the ground either dead or merely stunned. Surrounded by Federation guns, Avon looks into camera and smiles as the titles black out the screen. A single shot is heard, followed by a volley of gunfire.

'Blake' was completed between 5 and 7 September. After that, the production office closed for a second and final time. 'Rescue' had started Season Four with an audience of 7.8 million viewers, and the ratings hovered throughout the rest of the season at just below 9 million, which was the exact figure who tuned in to the most watched story of the run - titled, appropriately enough 'Blake'.

Surely, though, they couldn't have survived? Even with Blake himself present, they were facing impossible odds . . . But then, that was always the case . . . wasn't it?

The final moments. With Blake dead at his feet, Avon faces impossible odds, surrounded by Federation guards.

Season 4
Episode Guide

Season Four

Regular Cast Members

Avon – Paul Darrow
Vila – Michael Keating
Dayna – Josette Simon
Tarrant – Steven Pacey
Soolin – Glynis Barber
Voice of Orac and Slave – Peter Tuddenham
Servalan (Stories D3, D5, D7-D12) – Jacqueline Pearce

Regular Production Team

Producer – Vere Lorrimer
Script Editor – Chris Boucher

In 'Assassin', the Scorpio crew are one step ahead of Servalan.

D1: Rescue
Written by Chris Boucher.

Servalan has left Terminal lined with explosive traps, one of which kills Cally. Avon and the others move to higher ground to try and avoid any more fatalities, and come across the *Scorpio*, run by a salvage operator named Dorian. At gun point, Dorian complies and takes them to his base on the planet Xenon, where it's clear they were expected. His partner, Soolin, seems harmless, but Dorian has plans to absorb the lifeforce of both her and the *Liberator* crew.

Dorian – Geoffrey Burridge
The Creature – Rob Middleton
Director – Mary Ridge
Designer – Roger Cann
Broadcast: 28 September 1981 1920-2010hrs
Novelized by Trevor Hoyle in *Blake's 7 - Scorpio Attack*

D2: Power
Written by Ben Steed.

Trapped in Dorian's base, a device has been set to detonate and the only way out is on *Scorpio*, which even Vila can't break into. On the surface of Xenon, one by one the crew are captured by the Hommiks, an all-male race of savages at war with the female

'Stardrive'.

Seska. While Pella, leader of the three surviving Seska, tries to trick her way on board the *Scorpio* to flee the planet, Orac had deduced that a piece of jewellery she's wearing might be the key to getting the teleport system on *Scorpio* to work.

Gunn Sar – Dicken Ashworth
Pella – Juliet Hammond Hill
Nina – Jenny Oulton
Cato – Paul Ridley
Kate – Alison Glennie
Luxia – Linda Barr
Director – Mary Ridge
Designer – Roger Cann
Broadcast: 5 October 1981 1920-2010hrs

D3: Traitor

Written by Robert Holmes.

The *Scorpio* crew discover the Federation is using a pacifying drug to dominate the planet Helotrix. It is whilst trying to find an antidote for the formula being used on the Helots that Tarrant and Dayna see Servalan, who they thought had been killed when the *Liberator* was destroyed. Under the guise of Security Officer Sleer, she ruthlessly kills anyone who knows her as Servalan. Avon has to try and get Dayna and Tarrant away from the planet as the *Scorpio* is detected by the Federation, who start to pursue it.

Leitz – Malcolm Stoddard
Colonel Quute – Christopher Neame
Major Hunda – Robert Morris
Practor – John Quentin
Forbus – Edgar Wreford
General – Nick Brimble
The Tracer – David Quilter
Avandir – Neil Dickson
Sergeant Hask – Cyril Appleton
Igin – George Lee
Director – David Sullivan-Proudfoot
Designers – Roger Cann and Nigel Curzon
Broadcast: 12 October 1981 1920-2010hrs
Novelized by Trevor Hoyle in *Blake's 7 - Scorpio Attack*

Soolin joins Keiller in his control room in 'Gold'.

D4: Stardrive

Written by James Follett.

Stranded and carrying out repair work on the *Scorpio*, the crew see three Federation ships explode with no apparent cause. Slowing a replay down, they see it was an attack by Space Choppers, moving at an incredible speed. Orac concludes that they have the Photon Drive System that a Dr Plaxton was developing, so they head for the planet Casper and the lair of the psychotic Space Rats, whose resources she is using to work on the system. The *Scorpio* crew plan to use it on the *Scorpio* engines, but they have to overcome the Space Rats first.

Doctor Plaxton – Barbara Shelley
Atlan – Damien Thomas
Bomber – Peter Sands
Napier – Leonard Kavanagh
Director – David Sullivan-Proudfoot
Designers – Roger Cann and Nigel Curzon
Broadcast: 19 October 1981 1920-2010hrs
Novelized by Trevor Hoyle in *Blake's 7 - Scorpio Attack*

D5: Animals

Written by Allan Prior.

Tarrant and Dayna head for Bucol 2, where Dayna is stranded and attacked by strange creatures before being rescued by Justin, her former tutor. Justin is now a genetic engineer creating animal lifeforms that are capable of moving into areas of radiation dangerous to humans to carry out repair work, rescues, and so on. As *Scorpio* races back, now repaired from the attack that made Tarrant leave Dayna behind, Servalan arrives and captures Dayna, whom she starts to torture to find out the secrets of Justin's work.

Justin – Peter Byrne
Captain – William Lindsay
Borr – Max Harvey
Ardus – Kevin Stoney
Og – David Boyce
Director – Mary Ridge
Designers – Roger Cann and Graham Lough
Broadcast: 26 October 1981 1920-2010hrs

D6: Headhunter
Written by Roger Parkes.

Vila and Tarrant arrive on the planet Pharos to pick up Muller, who has created a powerful android, but his creation has turned on him and killed him. The *Scorpio* actually picks up the android, which has put Muller's severed head on its own body in an attempt to disguise its true identity. The android's plan is to gain entry to the Xenon base and steal Orac, for the combined power of itself and Orac would make them invincible.

Muller – John Westbrook
Vena – Lynda Bellingham
Technician – Douglas Fielding
Android – Nick Joseph
Voice – Leslie Nunnerley
Director – Mary Ridge
Designers – Roger Cann and Graham Lough
Broadcast: 2 November 1981 1920-2010hrs

D7: Assassin
Written by Rod Beacham.

The planet Domo acts as a centre of pirate slavery, where captured travellers are sold off at auction. The *Scorpio* crew heads there with the information that Servalan has hired an assassin, known as Cancer, to eliminate them. Avon favours taking the battle to Cancer, rather than let Cancer find them. Escaping from the surface with an elderly man called Nebrox and a dancer called Piri, the crew think they've captured the assassin, but he's merely an actor hired to trick them by the real C ancer.

Verlis – Betty Marsden
Nebrox – Richard Hurndall
Piri – Caroline Holdaway
Cancer – John Wyman
Benos – Peter Attard
Tok – Adam Blackwood
Servalan's Captain – Mark Barrett
Director – David Sullivan-Proudfoot and (uncredited) Vere Lorrimer
Designer – Ken Ledsham
Broadcast: 9 November 1981 1920-2010hrs

Like a twisted Kirk and Spock, surely Avon and Vila were one of the great double acts of science fiction?

D8: Games
Written by Bill Lyons.

On the planet Mecron II, Belkov runs the vast mining operation to extract feldon crystals from the planet's core. An obsessive, master games player, he's adapted his computer so that even the defence systems of the mines have become a game. Servalan arrives, determined to find out why the load of crystals have not met with Belkov's original estimates. He has stored a haul of them on an orbiting carrier ship, which the *Scorpio* crew plan to steal, but Belkov is not that easy to outwit.

Belkov – Stratford Johns
Gerren – David Neal
Guard – James Harvey
Gambit – Rosalind Bailey
Director – Vivienne Cozens
Designers – Eric Walmsley and Ken Ledsham
Broadcast: 16 November 1981 1920-2010hrs

D9: Sand
Written by Tanith Lee.

Servalan and her team of investigators arrive on the planet Virn to find out what happened to some Federation researchers stationed there, who have all disappeared after they discovered a unique energy source. The *Scorpio* arrives with its crew searching for the same source, and Tarrant becomes trapped on the planet's surface with Servalan. Meanwhile *Scorpio* faces hazardous atmospheric conditions, which makes it impossible to get Tarrant back. It's

then that Tarrant realizes that the sand that's closing in around the base seems to be alive . . .

Reeve – Stephen Yardley
Chasgo – Daniel Hill
Keller – Jonathan David
Servalan's Assistant – Peter Craze
Computer – Michael Gaunt
Director – Vivienne Cozens
Designers – Eric Walmsley and Ken Ledsham
Broadcast: 23 November 1981 1920-2010hrs

D10: Gold
Written by Colin Davies.

An old acquaintance of Avon called Keiller, who is the purser on a passenger ship called *Space Princess*, tells him about the secret load of gold he is transporting on board, and how he has a plan for the *Scorpio* crew to steal it. However, the scheme is all part of an elaborate trap being set by an outside party. Fully aware of this fact, the *Scorpio* crew carry out the robbery, and find out that the person manipulating Keiller all along has been, as Avon fully expected - Servalan.

Keiller – Roy Kinnear
Doctor – Anthony Brown
Woman Passenger – Dinah May
Pilot – Norman Hanley
Director – Brian Lighthill
Designer – Ken Ledsham
Broadcast: 30 November 1981 1920-2010hrs

D11: Orbit
Written by Robert Holmes.

Egrorian, a brilliant scientist long thought to be dead, is in hiding on the planet Malodar. He contacts the *Scorpio* crew, and Avon and Vila travel to the planet's surface in a shuttle, where the scientist offers them a weapon called a Tachyon Funnel in exchange for Orac. With little choice, as Egrorian will surely use the weapon to destroy the *Scorpio* if they do not comply, Avon agrees, but uses a fake replica of the computer in the transaction. Servalan proves to be behind the scheme, and as Avon and Vila try to leave in the shuttle, they find the excess weight will not allow them to break orbit. Avon begins to consider how much Vila weighs . . .

Egrorian – John Savident
Pinder – Larry Noble
Director – Brian Lighthill
Designer – Ken Ledsham
Broadcast: 7 December 1981 1920-2010hrs

D12: Warlord
Written by Simon Masters.

Avon calls a summit conference at the Xenon base, bringing together the five most powerful anti-Federation factions in order to pool their resources. Their aim is to try to mass-distribute the antidote to the suppressant drug that the Federation uses to pacify the planets they rule. However, Zukan, one of the most powerful warlords to attend the conference is under Servalan's control. He plants bombs throughout the Xenon base, which soon detonate and discharge a lethal virus into the air to kill off any survivors.

Zukan – Roy Boyd
Zeeona – Bobbie Brown
Finn – Dean Harris
Boorva – Simon Merrick
Chalsa – Rick James
Lod – Charles Augins
Mida – Brian Spink
Director – Viktors Ritelis
Designer – Paul Allen
Broadcast: 14 December 1981 1920-2010hrs

D13: Blake
Written by Chris Boucher.

With Servalan now aware of the location of the Xenon base, the *Scorpio* crew blow it up as they abandon it. Avon then reveals that he has found the leader to unite the rebel forces and defeat the Federation. On the planet Guada Prime, Orac has located the whereabouts of Blake, now working as a bounty hunter. As they near the planet, the *Scorpio* is attacked. Vila, Avon, Dayna, Soolin and Orac are beamed to safety, and Tarrant crash-lands the ship. He's rescued from the wreckage by Blake, who hands him over for a reward. Tarrant mistakes this action - which is really a test to see if he's suitable to join Blake's cause - for betrayal by Blake.

Series Conclusion
Believing Tarrant's words about his betrayal by Blake, Avon kills Blake just as Federation guards storm the area. One by one the *Scorpio* crew are shot, except for Avon, who is surrounded by guns and simply smiles as he stands over Blake's body .

Blake – Gareth Thomas
Deva – David Collings
Arlen – Sasha Mitchell
Klyn – Janet Lees Price
Director – Mary Ridge
Designer – Roger Cann
Broadcast: December 21st 1981 1920-2010hrs

Morris Barry as Wiler in the Season 2 story 'Killer'.

10 Selling the Myth

When you compare the output of merchandise issued in connection with *Blake's 7* with, for the sake of argument, *Doctor Who* or the trilogy of *Star Wars* films, in terms of the science fiction genre, the exploits of the *Liberator* crew do seem to have been sadly neglected. Nevertheless, during the programme's initial run, there were several items of note.

There have been several novels, both written independently and adaptations of episodes, with the most recent being a volume written by Avon himself, Paul Darrow, with *Avon - A Terrible Aspect*, which was issued in America. Keen to put his thoughts and ideas about the character on paper, Darrow had several talks with English-based publishing houses about the possibility of writing such a book, but although there was interest, nobody actually took up the idea. It was Citadel Press in the US who published the work in 1989. A paperback edition followed a couple of years later, which is available in specialist shops in the UK.

'Ultraworld's author, Trevor Hoyle, actually came to know Boucher and the production team because of his work novelizing early episodes of the series, and won a commission through submitting his own ideas to write for Season Three. The first of his books dealt with the first four episodes of Season One, and had a general title of just *Blake's 7*, which was issued by Sphere Books during 1978. The following year, a second volume followed, again dealing with Season One episodes, with *Blake's 7 - Project Avalon* dealing with the episode noted in the book's title, together with 'Seek-Locate-Destroy', 'Duel', 'Deliverance', and finally, 'Orac'.

Hoyle moved over to BBC Books for his final novelization so far, when the company issued *Blake's 7 - Scorpio Attack*, to tie in with the launch of Season Four. Like the first book, this dealt with the first four episodes of that season, omitting only the plotline of 'Power' from the narrative.

All three books have been issued as paperbacks, with the first and third also released in hardback editions.

Target Books compiled an episode guide for the series, issued in both hardback and paperback under the title of *Blake's 7 - The Programme Guide* in 1982. Tony Attwood also completed a novel, alongside writing the programme guide, trying to deal with what could have happened to the *Scorpio* crew after the seemingly fatal ambush at the finale of 'Blake'. *Blake's 7 - Afterlife* came out in 1984, and saw characters such as Servalan being reduced to mere cameo appearances before being abruptly killed off. A sequel was planned by Attwood under the title of 'Blake's 7 - State of Mind', but this was never issued.

Annuals, featuring both comic strips, text stories and generally inaccurate picture articles, were published for three consecutive years by World

Judy Buxton as Inga on the set of
Season Two's 'Hostage'.

Distributors, who had a long history of titles, including the *Doctor Who Annuals*. For *Blake's 7* those for 1978 and 1979 were relatively common with a wide circulation and print run. The rarest of the three annuals, however, came out in 1981, when Season Four was being screened. When it soon became apparent that there would definitely be no more series in production after that, the run of annuals for 1981 was drastically cut back.

The theme tune was issued by BBC Records during the broadcast of Season One, and has gone on to feature on countless compilations of both TV themes, and specifically science fiction themes, with cover versions recorded with varying degrees of success by numerous bands and orchestras. More interestingly, when BBC Records were issuing both LPs and cassettes of sound effects, one was released in 1980 under the title of BBC Sci-Fi Sound Effects, and had quite a number of tracks drawn from the Blake audio Fx archive. For those who collect such things, a licence was granted for the actual sheet music of the theme to be issued, complete with a photograph of the *Liberator* on the cover.

Marvel Comics UK division started publishing a *Blake's Seven Magazine*, again to coincide with the launch of Season Four. This lasted for twenty-three issues, with a couple of special publications alongside it, from October 1981 until August 1983, by which time it had become clear that there was little hope of the series ever starting production again.

For younger children and toy collectors, there were several items of interest, varying from a pair of

jigsaws - one showing the crew on the flight deck of the *Liberator*, and the other showing the exterior of the spacecraft itself - to a series of models of the *Liberator* (and even toy spaceships which bore no relation to the series, but simply had a sticker with the logo on the side). Surprisingly, no manufacturers saw the potential in making a version of the teleport bracelets or even the elegant guns from the *Liberator*, but a compact version of the guns used by Federation troopers was made available.

Making such items as these artefacts was up to the ingenuity of the viewer, and certainly with Season Four, the ever-reliable *Blue Peter* was on hand, with part of an episode spent showing the viewers how to make the new style of teleport bracelets used for the new episodes. There were no 'action figures' as such, like the vast array of *Star Wars* characters available, but quite some time after the series had finished, a company called Comet Miniatures did start a range of tiny metal figures based around the series.

For more personalized items on anyone from Blake to Soolin, fans who wrote to the production office always received a postcard of one of the characters requested, and sometimes a badge in addition to this, together with a standard reply. The badges have become highly collectable, and it was not unknown for one of the cast, if they had time to spare while waiting to see someone like Maloney or Lorrimer, to sit and just sign postcards, so a few fans were lucky enough to get an autograph as well.

There were also T-shirts, baseball caps, sew-on

In the early 1990s Sally Knyvette joined the cast of country soap, Emmerdale.

badges and posters, but surely the most requested and most collectable items were the actual programmes. Apart from the repeat run of the final episodes of the previous season prior to the start of a new run of episodes, *Blake's 7* was never given a proper repeat run as such, except for a repeat screening of Season Four, and remained unseen on television for quite a few years... In 1985, BBC Video started to issue the series, but in a heavily edited form.

The first volume had the general heading of 'The Beginning', which carried Season One's first four stories in a movie-length format, with dozens of scenes now cut. Two more volumes followed in 1986, with the headings of 'Duel', and 'Orac'. The first had material from Season One's sixth, seventh and ninth episodes, while the latter volume had the twelfth and thirteenth episodes of Season One, and the first episode of Season Two.

A fourth volume called 'Aftermath' was released in Australia first, before it reached the UK in 1990. It featured material taken from Season Three - the first two episodes and the ninth. Yet even though these tapes were produced there was still a growing demand for the complete and uncut series. Eventually, the BBC did start to release them, with a run of twenty-six tapes that took from 1991 to 1993 to complete. Each one had an artwork cover, and only Season One's second episode, 'Space Fall',

suffered from the editor's scissors, with a fight scene between Avon and one of the guards on the prison ship being slightly trimmed. Other than that, the series could now be seen as it was originally broadcast over ten years before.

In 1994, *Blake's 7* suddenly began to experience a renaissance as the UK-based cable channel, UK Gold, which relies on the vaults of the BBC and Thames Television for its programming, started to run the entire series. And towards the end of the year, Marvel Comics published a superb winter special, and thereafter began issuing a new series of poster magazines on a monthly basis, with articles from the research team behind Marvel's other acclaimed title, the *Doctor Who Magazine*. Their consummate, intelligent research promises to chronicle the making of the series as never before.

Suddenly the demand for the programme is there again. A whole new 'video' generation are discovering *Blake's 7*, and for the older fans, it's just as though it never went away.

The long-running *Blake's 7* fan club, HORIZON, is still thriving, having run since the series was actually still on air. Details are available from HORIZON, c/o Miss Ann Steele, 66 Sherwood Park Road, Sutton, Surrey SM1 2SG.

BOXTREE TITLES

0 7522 0959 0	THE DOCTORS - 30 YEARS OF TIME TRAVEL	£14.99
0 7522 0844 6	ALIENS TECHNICAL MANUAL	£13.99
1 85283 866 3	THE MAKING OF QUANTUM LEAP	£12.99
0 7522 0938 8	CAPTAINS LOGS SUPPLEMENTAL SEASON 7	£9.99
0 7522 0839 X	BEYOND UHURA: STAR TREK AND OTHER MEMORIES	£15.99
0 7522 0868 3	LOST VOYAGES OF TREK AND THE NEXT GENERATION	£9.99
1 85283 340 8	STAR TREK NEXT GENERATION TECHNICAL MANUAL	£13.99
1 85283 398 X	TREK: UNIVERSAL INDEX	£9.99
0 7522 0859 4	GUIDE TO THE STAR WARS UNIVERSE	£8.99
0 7522 0887 X	STAR WARS TECHNICAL JOURNAL	£14.99

All these books are available at your bookshop or can be ordered direct from the publisher. Just tick the titles you want and fill in the form below.

Prices and availability subject to change without notice.

Boxtree Cash Sales, P.O. Box 11, Falmouth, Cornwall TR10 9EN.
Please send cheque or postal order for the value of the book and add the following for postage and packing:

U.K. including BFPO – £1.00 for one book, plus 50p for the second book, and 30p for each additional book ordered up to £3.00 maximum.

OVERSEAS including Eire – £2.00 for the first book, plus £1.00 for the second book, and 50p for each additional book ordered.

OR please debit this amount from my Access/Visa Card (delete as appropriate)

Card number

Amount £

Expiry Date on card

Signed

Name

Address